TSUNAMI

TSUNAMI

Building Organizations Capable of Prospering in Tidal Waves

Victor Pinedo

iUniverse, Inc.

New York Lincoln Shanghai

TSUNAMI
Building Organizations Capable of Prospering in Tidal Waves

iUniverse books may be ordered through booksellers or by contacting:

iUniverse
2021 Pine Lake Road, Suite 100
Lincoln, NE 68512
www.iuniverse.com
1-800-Authors (1-800-288-4677)

ISBN-13: 978-0-595-30655-8 (pbk)
ISBN-13: 978-0-595-75792-3 (cloth)
ISBN-13: 978-0-595-75485-4 (ebk)
ISBN-10: 0-595-30655-1 (pbk)
ISBN-10: 0-595-75792-8 (cloth)
ISBN-10: 0-595-75485-6 (ebk)

Printed in the United States of America

I dedicate this book to my wonderful wife, Magaly, and our son, Victor Joseph. They were always there for me during its writing, and they gave me tremendous support. They also sacrificed most, because of the time I spent writing instead of being with them. Also, to Paul Guinn for the countless hours he spent challenging, discussing, and refining with me the concepts and content of this book: for his encouragement and for his unconditional support.

Contents

Acknowledgments

Many people helped make this book a reality:

My grandmother, Sarah Cohen Henríquez, who said to me many years ago, "*No,* you already have; *yes,* you can always get." She meant that we must ask for what we want; no one should settle for the status quo. This led to my search for ways to help people find a more egalitarian and prosperous way of life, even in times when economic and political tidal waves are crashing into our world.

My friend Harry Lasker, who pioneered with me the early research in Curaçao. His research proved there were ways to help companies and communities mature and become healthier.

Maureen (KiKi) McShane, who cofounded Corporate Transitions with me. Her ideas, contributions, and hard work were important in bringing these theories to life.

Francisco Loschiavo, who is in charge of Corporate Transitions in Brazil. Through constant challenge, he helped sharpen my ideas and concepts, and helped ground them more firmly in reality. He was also the driving force behind several articles that were important predecessors to this book. His friendship and insightful knowledge of theories that support Organizational Architecture unfolded into a constant relationship of mutual growth and respect, while the theories and their application evolved over the years.

Paul Tolchinsky and Performance Development Associates, for our lively and productive debates as we integrated Organizational Architecture and the Whole-Scale approach.

Corporate Transitions Brazil, whose members included Francisco Loschiavo, Ariolino de Andrade, Ronald Z. Carvalho, Guilherme Sztutman, Els Moerman, Maria Luiza Paiva, and Luiz Carlos Teixeira de Freitas. Without their teamwork, the Portuguese edition of this book would never have reached its final form. Special thanks to Luiz Carlos who spent so many hours with me to bring the Portuguese edition closer to Brazil's social reality. Thanks also to Guilherme and Ronald for the final integration of the book. Thanks to Maria Luiza for spreading the word about the book's existence in Brazil, Andrade for his constant advice and research, and Els for coordinating the complicated agenda of cross-border citizens.

Wolmer Moreira da Silveira deserves special mention for insisting that this book become part of Brazilian business literature.

I cannot forget all the clients who trusted me with their companies, and who were innovative enough to make this approach a part of their own basic beliefs, in particular, Shaunny Abeyta (who spent many hours on the phone with me discussing these concepts) and Rick Ghio (a steadfast friend and champion of our approach). I also want to thank Paulo Villares (our first client in Brazil) and Alvaro Resteno. Ricardo Young Silva, who wrote the foreword of the Brazilian edition, was the CEO of the first Brazilian company I worked with forming a near global merger. Thanks also to the Bottom Line team, who as well as being a client, cocreated the book's cover.

I also want to thank Paulo Villares, Fernando Hilsenbeck, Mario Noberto, Fernando Moureau, Andre Kauffman, and Clovis Carvalho for the hours they spent reading and criticizing the manuscripts.

Finally, I want to recognize Jane Loevinger, Ichak Adizes, and George Land for the important influence that their theories of had on my thinking throughout the years.

A Special Word from the Author

This book was first published in Brazil in October 2003 and then in the United States in February 2004. I used the *tsunami* concept as a metaphor for the dangerous business and economic environment that our organizations and socioeconomic systems were facing. The idea behind the book was to help forward-thinking individuals become aware that these societal and organizational tsunamis existed and to give them tools to prepare their organizations and societies to survive them.

I had read how destructive tsunamis could be and had seen photographs of their power and horrific effect. However, I had never dreamt that in my lifetime I would actually witness such a destructive event. Yet, to my horror, on December 26, 2004, I watched a tsunami strike the Indian Ocean basin, killing a quarter of a million people and wiping out entire populations.

At the time of this appalling disaster, both translations of this book were scheduled for a second printing, while a Spanish edition was ready to go to press. I seriously considered holding off the new editions. I did not want the book, with its suddenly notorious title, to appear opportunistic, taking advantage of the pain of others. I did not want it to come out until everyone had a chance to work through the physical and psychological wounds caused by catastrophe the world had witnessed (and that some had lived through). I even considered finding a new metaphor to describe the perilous business environment confronting our organizations and societies.

Then in the World Economic Forum in Davos, Switzerland, in late January, President George Chirac of France made a speech that changed my mind. In it, he said:

> The tidal wave that recently devastated the Indian Ocean, the first major natural disaster of the twenty-first century, is an indicator of the state of this world of ours…The scale of the destruction is a reminder of the fragil-

ity of humankind in the face of nature. It calls for our urban and highly technological civilization to show greater humility, respect and responsibility...*This disaster should raise the alarm, because our world suffers chronically from what has been strikingly called the "silent tsunamis"* [my italics]. Famine. Infectious diseases that decimate the life force of entire continents. Violence and revolt. Regions given over to anarchy. Uncontrolled migratory movements. Rises in extremism, breeding grounds for terrorism.

Chirac's *silent tsunamis* are caused by principles similar to the *business tsunamis* that I write about in this book. As I read his speech and also other articles about the disaster, I realized that the tsunami metaphor was timely and important. President Chirac said that societies should be learning from what happened in the Indian Ocean; the business community must also search for solutions to create better organizations and a more secure business environment.

Today more than ever, the situations and solutions I present in this book are important for us to build organizations that are better prepared to deal with the tsunamis that hit us in our businesses and communities. This will ultimately help to create a business climate that will have fewer and fewer tsunamis in it. A more secure business climate will then lead to a more secure social climate and a better world for all.

I hope that this book will give you ideas that will help you, your companies, and your communities find the ingredients that you need to create organizations and societies that can successfully survive tidal waves.

Delray Beach, Florida

February 6, 2005

Foreword

During the 1980s and 1990s, several organizational theories promised the miracle of competitiveness. Consultants helped top management increase productivity and decrease cost through reengineering, outsourcing, and total quality certification. These theories, directed at improving existing company processes, helped companies increase short-term productivity, but they contributed nothing toward sustainable agility and competitiveness.

Our new globalized world represents a marked increase in the complexity of the business environment, which requires organizations to think differently. Most current organizational theories can no longer handle the complexity of the world market. Companies now operate in an environment where knowledge determines their survivability. Furthermore, companies' societal roles have also changed radically. *Are managers prepared to respond competently to these challenges?*

Colleges and MBA programs do not prepare managers for this new business world. There has been a shift in the competencies that leaders need. Even a thorough understanding of technology and management theory is no longer enough in the modern management environment.

To survive, twenty-first century companies have to become organic, flexible, adaptable, and intelligent. Einstein said that it is impossible to solve a problem from within the same theoretical framework that originated it. Thus, it is impossible to solve the management crisis that organizations are experiencing today using classic management concepts. Hierarchical organizations, strongly structured and centered on productivity and the generation of wealth for their shareholders alone, are under serious risk of petrification. The key to organizational survivability now involves a fundamental reexamination of purpose and values, as well as a rethinking of the corporate structure.

Today's companies hold enormous power. The social role once played by the Church and the State has been taken over by organizations, whether for-

or non-profit. Their economic resources represent 60 to 70 percent of the world economy. What these organizations decide to do and how they do it molds the structure of society. Considering the precarious nature of the current world economy, it seems that our managerial and political decisions have failed more than they have succeeded. To face this challenge, organizations urgently need a new management concept.

In this book, Victor Pinedo brings us encouraging new ideas and methods to change the way things are. First, he invites all stakeholders to structure their organizations based on the new realities of globalization. Second, he shows us how people who are motivated, participative, and committed are able to work intelligently, guaranteeing the survivability of organizations in the complex societies of today's information age.

Victor strongly opposes rigid organizational hierarchies because the more hierarchically structured organizations are, the less capable they are of changing. However, this is common knowledge. His innovation is in revealing that by discouraging decision making at the bottom, hierarchical structures alienate those at the top. This causes and preserves immaturity in the members of the organization, making them easy to manipulate. It also creates frustration and anger, which the members may eventually turn against the company and indeed against society.

Victor shows us that the only way that companies can achieve the motivation, creativity, strength, and agility they need to adapt to a violently changing environment is through cocreation of a new organization. He often speaks about how *culture sucks*, meaning that the current managerial culture is powerful enough to sabotage any attempt to change. Many companies embark on change programs only to find, after spending significant effort and resources on the process, that nothing has really changed. Simply improving existing processes is not enough. Unless the company changes its fundamental structure, its DNA, all attempts to improve will eventually fail.

To succeed, change must happen from the foundations to the top, actively involve all stakeholders, and reach deeply into the company's values system. Building a house without understanding how it will work or codesigning it with those that will live in it will render it useless and displease everyone.

Today more than ever, companies are important vehicles for continuous individual development, and are socially accountable agents of change in the market and society. This new and important role requires maturity from company leaders and stakeholders. Today's business community must rethink its values and means of achieving economic development. The willful exploitation of resources combined with the devaluation of those that work within it is chipping away at the foundations of modern society. We simply cannot sit idly and watch this happen.

In this book, Victor Pinedo shows us how to create social and business maturity, reassessing humans as a source of creation and renewal. He shows us the way to create the new organizations that will lead us into a new, brighter future.

Ricardo Young
President of the ETHOS Institute
President of Yázigi-InterNexus

Chapter 1

It All Started in Curaçao

Suddenly, surprisingly, the tsunami arrived. Distant, dull sounds preceded a tower-ing wave that destroyed entire cities, drowning men, women, and children. Born in the deepest layers of the ocean floor, the powerful wave left few survivors: only those who had learned to predict tidal waves, who had sailboats designed to survive them, and who had the ability to sail through them.

This book is a brief record of theories and practices over the last three decades, based on my experience as a business manager, psychologist, and advocate of change in complex organizations. It is intended to help companies and corporations prepare for a new world—a world in which we already live, which presents us with many new challenges.

I will present an integrated method for designing and applying improve-ments to production, management, and business processes. More importantly, I will introduce a new organizational model, aimed at transforming the inter-action among organizations, their stakeholders[1], and entire societies.

This presentation of Organizational Architecture[2] will be a practical refer-ence as well as a theoretical work that professional managers and implement-ers of organizational transformation processes can easily put into practice.

---

1. The term *stakeholder* has been used in the entire book in its contempo-rary conception as *interested party* (shareholders, employees, suppliers, customers, and segments of society), rather than limited to those that retain the capital (stockholders).
2. Organizational Architecture is an international trademark of Corporate Transitions International and the author's copyright.

What Are Tsunamis?

I have chosen to title this book *Tsunami*, a word the *Merriam-Webster Dictionary* (2003) defines as "a great sea wave produced by submarine earth movement." Tsunamis are fundamentally different from storm waves caused by storm winds. People and organizations can easily predict storm waves and can prepare for them. Tsunamis, on the other hand, are caused by sudden shifts in the ocean floor that move rapidly and are almost undetected until they thunder over the land, destroying everything with their fearsome power.

Tsunamis also happen in the business world. They are the destructive waves of socioeconomic change that come from sudden, fundamental shifts in belief structures, that move rapidly and almost undetected until they destroy companies, economies, and entire societies.

A Tsunami in Curaçao

What follows is the story of how my colleagues and I discovered these tsunamis, and the ways that your organization can prepare for and even avoid them.

There was a time, thirty years ago, when I lived peacefully on the Caribbean island of Curaçao in the Dutch Antilles, my place of birth. I enjoyed that corner of paradise, managing my family's business concerns (a Coca-Cola bottling plant, an ice-cream factory, a soap works, a chocolate candy factory, a dairy products plant, a catering service, and other businesses). I was also vice president of my country's Chamber of Industry and Commerce and the governor of the Lions' Club of the Caribbean and Northern South America. I had just received a master's degree in psychology, and I was doing postgraduate studies in business administration. My entire future lay in front of me, and I sincerely believed in my model of the world.

That world crumbled one day in May 1969. A series of social upheavals, triggered by popular protests, resulted in riots that culminated in burning large parts of our capital city and devastating damage to my country.

It started when Shell Oil laid off two thousand workers from its local oil refinery, the result of downsizing. Shell offered to bring back many of them as employees of third-party outsourcing companies, but at substantially lower wages than they had received before the layoff. Dissatisfied and angry, the workers started a picket line in front of the refinery. By dusk, they were marching toward the city with flaming torches and protest banners. People who were watching the march spontaneously joined it. As it grew, the march became increasingly violent. The marchers began looting shops and supermarkets along the way.

Soon the increasingly violent mob approached its objective, Willemstad City Hall. The National Guard was deployed to protect City Hall; in the excitement a soldier shot down one of the leaders. This triggered a full-scale riot. The rioters began burning the city.

From my perch at the top of a hill, I watched my hometown go up in flames. I was in agony. The raw hatred that I had seen on the faces of the protesters seared my soul, just as the flames of their torches seared Willemstad. The tragic uprising reduced an important part of my beliefs to ashes. A tsunami had just destroyed my world—a huge wave born of a sudden shift in the basis of the social and business environments of Curaçao, ending in the near-destruction of an entire socioeconomic system.

Why had this happened? For the people of Curaçao to burn down half of their capital city, there had to be something fundamentally wrong with the corporate models being used, and indeed the entire social structure. My colleagues and I conducted a long period of research and analysis dedicated to understanding the causes of the riot of May 30. By working with the leaders of the rebellion, we were better able to understand the reason it all happened.

We discovered that the uprising was not simply because of dissatisfaction over wages or working conditions. Rather, the cause was the population's built-up anger and frustration against an excessively hierarchical society.

Over the years, we have continued to study this phenomenon. We have watched our world become more global, and we have seen many business and political tsunamis. Some recent examples include General Electric (and Jack Welch), Tyco (and Kozlowski, Walsh, Swartz, Belnick), WorldCom, the Andersen trial, Enron, Merrill Lynch, ImClone (and Martha Stewart), the Wall Street Probe, Global Crossing, Adelphia, Royal Ahold, and even Bin Laden and September 11.

These events have a common cause: the hierarchical, elitist value system, the belief that some people are naturally better than others, and all that this implies. This naturally creates frustration and anger in those at the lower levels of the hierarchy, which only proves the need for hierarchy in the minds of those at the top. This results in a stronger hierarchy and still more frustration and anger. This cycle repeats and reinforces itself, as it did in Curaçao until it brought about the tsunami that destroyed so much of Willemstad. As our world has become more global, this cycle has emerged in companies, in countries, and even between regions (for example, the First World versus Third World phenomenon).

Hierarchical elitism is immature behavior. Because immature individuals are dependent on their environment (as opposed to being in control of it) for the satisfaction of their needs, they find the rigid structures of hierarchy protective and comforting. They also find the rigid structures appealing, especially elitist structures, because they see them as a way to gain personal power and advantage over others. Thus, hierarchical elitism is inherently unproductive, because it encourages "every man for himself" behavior.

More mature individuals are interdependent and cooperative, and they see achievement in terms of the organization rather than the individual. Their structures are less hierarchical and more egalitarian. Thus, they are much more productive. Where does mature behavior come from then? How do individuals and organizations mature?

Abraham Maslow (1954) speaks of a continuum of needs that individuals have to satisfy before they can reach full maturity or self-actualization. These are:

- Physical needs

- The need for security

- The need to belong or to be accepted

- The need to achieve

- Self-realization needs

Each of these needs forms an arena in which individuals have to prove themselves if they are to develop to a higher consciousness level. If they succeed, for example, at the *physical needs* level, they can move on to the next proving ground, the arena of *security needs*. If they do not succeed in satisfying their physical needs, they go on automatic pilot (continuously showing behavior associated with satisfying physical needs) as they go through life.

In Curaçao my colleagues and I also discovered the work of Dr. Jane Loevinger. She has shown that, although all human beings have the potential to mature, some would stop maturing (stagnate) at certain points in their development. Stagnation inevitably results in feelings of frustration and anger, and, as we have seen, these emotions can cause the sudden shocks that end in tsunamis. Loevinger (1970) developed an instrument that can measure the point at which a person has stopped developing and what behavior and value system we can expect from an individual at that stage.

Dr. Loevinger identified six levels or stages of maturity:

1. Impulsive

2. Self-protective

3. Conformist

4. Conscientious

5. Autonomous

6. Integrated

Loevinger characterized each level using four dimensions: impulse control, interpersonal style, cognitive style, and conscious preoccupation. Note that most people do not match a single level completely. I describe a person being at a particular stage depending on how closely his or her four characteristic dimensions fit that stage. A person's level of maturity can be anywhere on the spectrum, even between levels. Thus, the ego levels are simply well-understood points in a continuous spectrum of human maturity. I will discuss Dr. Loevinger's work in more detail in Chapter 3.

I also discovered the work of Dr. Julian B. Rotter (1966), who talks about the "locus of control." This also describes a spectrum. At one end are people who feel that they are the *creators* of their future, and at the other are people who feel that they are *creatures* of fate. A person can be at any point in the spectrum, based on his or her creature/creator feelings. I will discuss Dr. Rotter's work in more detail in Chapter 5.

The research my colleagues and I completed included plotting Loevinger's ego stages against Rotter's feelings of creature/creator. Based on our results, we came up with the following picture.

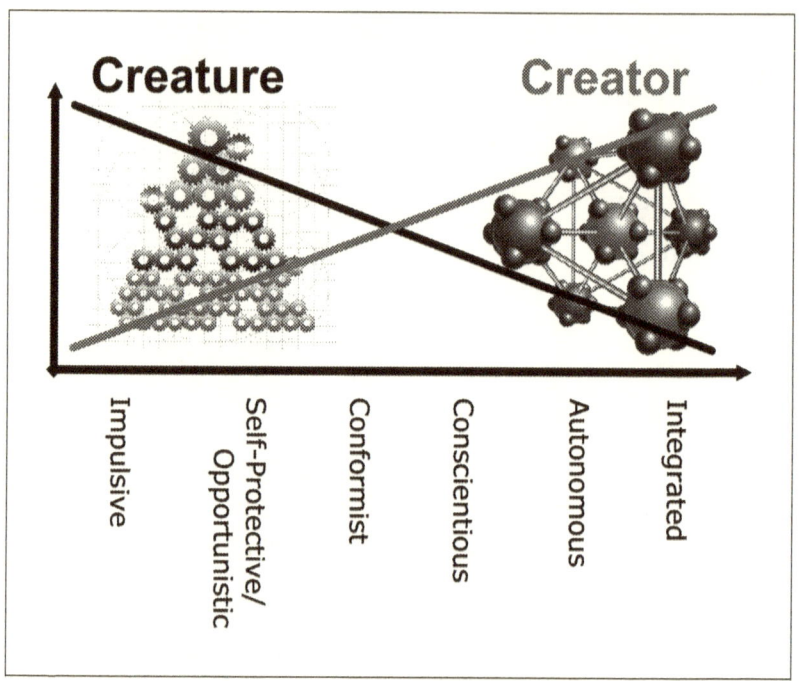

Figure 1: Creature/creator feelings at different maturity stages

Figure 1 shows the various stages of maturity plotted against how strongly the individual feels that he or she is a creature or a creator. Note that the creature sentiment is highest in immature individuals who have stagnated early in their development and who show impulsive or self-protective (that I refer to hereafter as opportunistic) behavior. It is at its lowest at the more mature stages such as conscientious, autonomous, and integrated. The feeling of being a creator, on the other hand, is lowest at the impulsive level and the highest at the integrated level.

The research we did in Curaçao gave us a practical understanding of the causes of tsunamis in a business organization. Our research showed that most people in the Curaçao population were at the opportunistic or conformist consciousness level, according to Loevinger's descriptions.

Another important finding in the Curaçao studies regards the high degree of correlation between maturity and ethical behavior. The studies carried out by Harvard professor Lawrence Kohlberg clearly show that the ethical behavior of individuals progresses as they change through the successive stages of maturity. This compares well to the models proposed by Maslow, Rotter, and Loevinger.

Kohlberg's model (1981), backed by behavioral psychology research, has six stages divided into three distinct levels, as shown in Table 1.

Level	Stage	Social Outlook
Preconventional	1	Obedience or punishment
	2	Opportunist morality
Conventional	3	Morality in search of social acceptance
	4	Internalizes law and order
Postconventional	5	Accepts interdependence
	6	Respects universal principles

Table 1: Stages of Moral Maturity

Clearly, the preconventional morality level governs the impulsive and opportunistic stages, whereas the conventional morality level characterizes Loevinger/Pinedo-Lasker's conformist and self-perceptive stages. Note that only Loevinger's conscientious and autonomous stages correlate with Kohlberg's most advanced postconventional morality level. Table 2 shows this correlation.

Moral stage	Ego stage
Punishment and obedience	Impulsive
Instrumental exchange	Opportunist
Interpersonal conformity	Conformist
Law and order	Conscientious
Prior rights and social contract	Autonomous
Universal ethical principles	Integrated

Table 2: How Moral Stages Relate to Ego Stages

The following describes each of Kohlberg's three levels and six stages of moral development, including the individual's motivation to behave in a certain way at each stage:

Premoral or Preconventional Level

Stage 1: Punishment and Obedience. Behavior is motivated by the anticipation of pleasure or pain.

Stage 2: Instrumental Exchange. Individuals pursue their own interests, but let others do the same. What is right involves equal exchange.

Conventional Morality Stages

Stage 3: Interpersonal Conformity. Individuals value trust, caring, and loyalty to others as a basis for moral judgments

Stage 4: Law and Order. Moral judgments are based on the social order, law, justice, and duty

Postconventional or Principled Morality Stages

Stage 5: Prior Rights and Social Contract. Individuals reason that values, rights, and principles form the basis of or transcend the law.

Stage 6: Universal Ethical Principles. An individual who reaches this stage acts out of universal principles based on the equality and worth of all human life.

Kohlberg came to some interesting conclusions:

- Stage development is invariant.

- Subjects cannot comprehend moral reasoning at a stage more than one stage beyond their own.

- Individuals are cognitively attracted to reasoning one level above their own present predominant level.

- People move toward the next stage when they experience cognitive disequilibrium, that is, when their current cognitive outlook is not adequate to cope with a given moral dilemma.

- It is possible for a person to be physically mature and morally [and emotionally] immature.

Our Curaçao studies showed a direct connection between each of Kohlberg's stages of moral development and Loevinger's stages of maturity. They showed that people who have stopped maturing at Loevinger's impulsive or opportunistic stages are preconventional according to Kohlberg and so are constantly protecting themselves against punishment. They obey only because they are afraid of losing what little feelings of security they still have. At the conformist level, where people want to be accepted, morality equals conformity. People are motivated to behave in ways that will gain the approval of their peers. At the more mature levels (conscientious, autonomous, and integrated), law, order, rights, social responsibility, and universal ethical principles emerge.

These findings were important as my colleagues and I began designing the programs and processes that were later to become Organizational Architecture, the discipline discussed in this book. They gave us important insights into the structures and skills that managers would need to move their organizations to higher levels of maturity and behavior that is more ethical.

Although I will discuss Loevinger's ego stage model in more depth in Chapter 3, it is important to note two significant points in the maturity spectrum. The first is the transition between the opportunistic and conformist phases, and the second is the transition between conscientious and autonomous phases. As I shall show later, the former is worthy of note because of its contribution to tsunamis in organizations and societies, and the latter because of its importance to the survival of these same organizations and societies.

At the opportunistic-conformist transitional stage, thinking is black and white, and win and lose. People consider others to be "with them" or "against them." People who are at the opportunistic-conformist transition like to follow standards and feel shame only if discovered blatantly breaking rules. They do not question rules (especially those made by heroes or gurus) and identify with them. They desire to belong to a respected group with whom they identify. They feel themselves to be creatures of fate, fulfilling the ideas of others. They have little or no sense of personal control over their life or environment.

At the conscientious-autonomous transitional stage, a person's thinking is more mature. These personalities follow rules that agree with their consciences. They believe in the creativity and interdependence of human beings. They like to set and achieve their own goals. They will not accept injustice to themselves or their colleagues. They listen to and respect others, and they demand respect for their own ideas. They think independently and identify with people who have earned their respect. They believe that they can develop their own ideas and find creative solutions for problems that come up. They feel that they have power over their environment and are largely the creators of their own destiny.

This discovery became especially important when my colleagues and I related it to David McClelland's studies on social motives.

Achievement Motivation, Powerlessness, and Maturity

McClelland's book titled *The Achieving Society* (1961) powerfully expresses the relationship between individual psychological patterns and social change. After years of psychological research, McClelland was able to identify several fundamental human motives:

- The power motive

- The affiliation motive

- The achievement motive

McClelland said that, depending on his or her motivation, an individual will display different kinds of behavior and have different concerns. For example, my colleagues and I found that power-motivated individuals exhibited opportunistic and defensive behavior. Power-motivated people are interested mainly in controlling others in the process of seeking their own ends. This behavior is inefficient and counterproductive, especially from the organizational point of view.

On the other hand, affiliation-motivated people are primarily interested in interaction with others, expressing feelings and ideas, and getting others' approval. They are happiest when they feel appreciated and when they have the opportunity for inter-personal contact. This behavior, from the organizational point of view, is not as destructive or harmful as the power-motivated behavior, but people who are motivated primarily by what others think of them are unable to think and act strategically (and thus lack maturity).

McClelland found that the achievement motive related strongly to socio-economic development. It causes feelings of satisfaction. Achievement-motivated individuals, in contrast to the other two types, are interested in successfully carrying out tasks. They have the desire to organize individually and collectively for task fulfillment. They exhibit professional excellence and rational problem solving, and have a tendency to be efficient and productive. McClelland developed an educational methodology designed to stimulate and heighten the achievement motive.

The author's research with McClelland's motives found that they are, in fact, crude predictors of Loevinger's ego levels. Achievement motivation is one characteristic of a more mature individual, whereas affiliation motivation is a sign of conformist behavior. People with strong power motivation are usually at a lower (i.e. impulsive or opportunistic) level of ego development. They do not respond to achievement-motivation training because it requires more emotional maturity and intellectual abilities than they have yet developed.

In Curaçao (and everywhere else in the world, as we later discovered), people become trapped at low maturity levels and function there.

One of the characteristics of the lower ego stages (impulsive, opportunistic, and conformist) is a hierarchical belief system. This helps people disguise their own powerlessness—even from themselves. People at the opportunistic and conformist stages need acceptance from others before they can accept themselves. If they feel unaccepted by others, they compensate by trying to become better than those who do not accept them. They start playing power games, such as seeking status and gaining material possessions. They believe that this will make the others accept them.

From the outside, this makes them look powerful. However, at some level they know that people are still accepting them only for their position in the power structure or for their possessions and so remain dissatisfied. Lacking any other means of gaining acceptance, they strive for more and more status (or possessions) but always fail to satisfy their need for acceptance.

Hierarchical beliefs say that some people are born to be leaders and some are born to be followers. They create status seeking and corporate ladder climbing. Those on top strive to secure their position and to make sure that those on the bottom never get on top. They feel, consciously or unconsciously, that if they can keep the people under them downtrodden and emotionally immature, they can keep control and thus get the best that their world has to offer. This has caused companies to institutionalize immaturity.

Those at the bottom, also having internalized the hierarchical values system, feel that if they do well in their lowly positions they may make it to the top in the next job (or next life). This belief system has led us to structure our lives hierarchically.

The problem with the hierarchical system is that it creates much frustration and anger. A hierarchical structure keeps most people from doing better, no matter how hard they work or how well they do. Even their rewards correlate to their position in the hierarchy. This frustration causes the tsunamis that I discussed earlier.

Imagine the hierarchical belief structure as a system of intermeshed gears, as shown in Figure 2. The gear on top is big and represents the big boss (the chief, the king, the CEO). Smaller gears below support those above. Each gear rests on another, smaller one and so forth until the bottom layer where the smallest gears are. I call the small gears *dumpies*. In a hierarchical organization, there is only room for one big gear, a few vice big gears, and many, many dumpies.

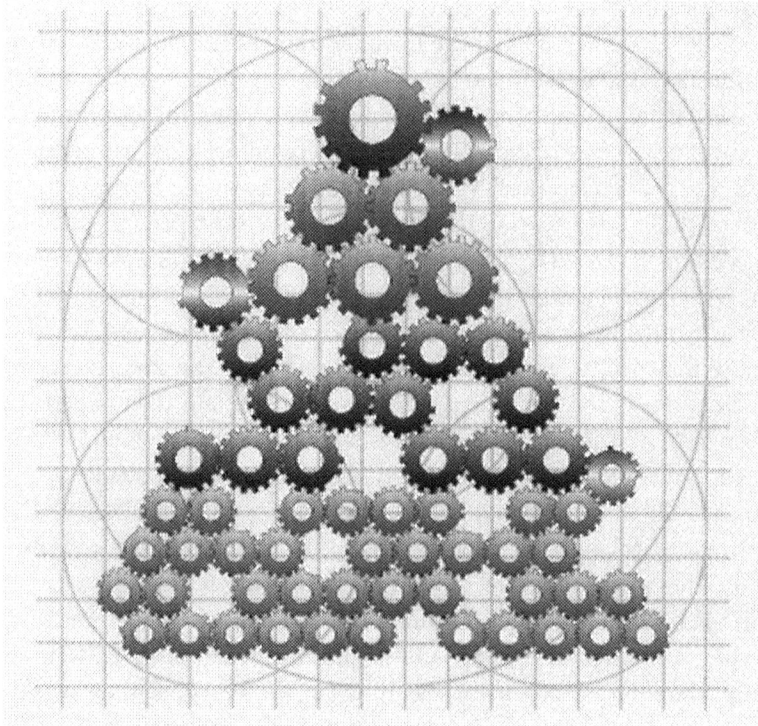

Figure 2: The elitist hierarchical values system in operation.

Imagine the big gear turning one complete turn. This would make the little gears—the dumpies—spin like crazy! Thus, when the head of a hierarchy makes a decision, everyone rushes around to carry it out without knowing why they are rushing around, only that the big gear said to. When the little gears spin, they get dizzy. In an organization, the dumpies' spinning is their frenetic efforts to carry out the latest whim of the big gear. Spinning makes them feel bad not only because it makes them dizzy, but because their powerlessness to stop the spinning makes them feel out of control!

To block these bad feelings, they go on what I call autopilot. A pilot who puts his or her airplane on autopilot does not have to do any thinking to fly the plane. People who go on autopilot, as I describe here, quit trying to think for themselves and just do what the bigger gears tell them to do. In order to survive in their job, they block all their emotions. They feel neither sad nor happy, but at least they can continue. I have seen many cases where a company's employees are on autopilot. They just show up for work and go through the motions. When five o'clock comes, they rush out the door. Unfortunately, this makes them terribly unproductive when compared to self-guided employees.

Autopilot also keeps them from having any challenges to overcome; therefore they can have no successes. As I said earlier, both are necessary for a person to become more mature. Without the opportunity to become more mature, that person stagnates emotionally.

In addition, even though they are on autopilot, they cannot help remembering their powerlessness, and this causes anger. They are reminded of their powerlessness every day. The anger builds like the pressures on the ocean floor. Then one day something happens to the system, and suddenly they release all that anger-energy at once. This creates a tsunami.

Power hierarchies cause immature behavior to continue. Studies have shown (and I will explore this in more detail later) that immature behavior, as I described as the opportunistic-conformist stage, inevitably leads to demotivation, low productivity, financial losses, and bankruptcies. It also leads to circumstances where astute, immature people can easily manipulate other immature people for their own advantage. A recent example is the CFO of a large telecommunications company that recently built a fifteen-million-dollar house even though his company was going into bankruptcy. There is Hugo Chavez's sudden rise to power in Venezuela and its resulting social turmoil. Also, let us never forget the deaths of thousands of innocent people that Osama bin Laden orchestrated. All these are the outcome of hierarchical values systems and beliefs.

Hierarchical values would have us believe that immaturity is unavoidable. Some are born to be rich, and some are born to be poor. Some have the genes of maturity, and some are doomed to be immature for life. It is not just companies that promote this belief. Societies do, too—and this is true globally. For example, over the centuries we have invented a First World and a Third world: global haves and have-nots; big gears and dumpies.

However, is immaturity unavoidable and unchangeable? Do we need power hierarchies just to deal with permanently immature employees? Is it possible to help individuals and organizations to mature? The studies my colleagues and I conducted in Curaçao showed that it is indeed possible to restart and even accelerate the maturation process in individuals, organizations, and societies. This is good news! Companies and societies that remain immature will be helpless against tsunamis and will eventually suffer socioeconomic decline, but those that become mature will thrive in this globalized world.

To survive and to prosper in the turbulent environment of the third millennium, companies need to respond as healthy, living organisms, with adaptability, speed, and precision never before necessary. This strategy will make their brands more competitive, guaranteeing their growth, revenue, and survivability.

In corporations, rigid hierarchical values produce inefficiency, sluggish response, and reactive (as opposed to proactive) behavior. As I have said before, this leads to attitudes—whether conscious or not—of hostility against the company, often revealed as absenteeism, procrastination, disloyalty, lack of commitment, and even sabotage.

Rigid hierarchies, nevertheless, continue to create more and more layers of "inferiors" in companies and corporations (management versus shop floor). Globalization only makes obvious the distance between those who live at the top and those who live at the bottom. This polarization has demanded increasingly stronger (even if inefficient) control methods to ensure the preservation of order and continuity of production.

There are clear similarities between the destructive events in Curaçao and those happening all over the world. I am certain of the need to give organizations a way to survive these enormous tsunami waves—a new sailboat and new sailing skills, if you will. Organizations need structural transformations if they are to improve competitiveness, working conditions, and the ability to survive disastrous changes. Only by creating a new class of organization can we create a harmonious, productive business environment, ensuring our own well-being on personal, professional, social, and civilization levels.

Organizations need something more than process refinement, empowerment, reengineering, or downsizing. These and other similar management modernization schemes are limited to refurbishing or readapting models from the past that can only work in outdated structures. The new environment calls for a new organization to cope with this new corporate and collective reality.

The newly reborn corporation will expand outward and upward, reaching the productivity, profitability, and competitiveness targets. It will simultaneously spread personal and managerial maturity to all stakeholders through deep analysis of the internal and external environment and their production and business processes.

My experience with transforming organizations has shown the benefits of replacing rigid, obsolescent power hierarchies with more agile, competitive, effective, and mature organic organizational structures. It has also shown the benefits of having more mature employees within such an organization, and I have seen how important it is to coordinate the company's improvement with the personal growth of its members. By simultaneously transforming the organization and the men and women that work within it, the knowledge, skills, and information the people gain will increase the productivity, sustainable profitability, ethical behavior, social responsibility, and organic nature of the organization.

The Global Stage

In the 1970s and 1980s, my colleagues and I developed a management method that helped transform hierarchical values systems into organic ones. As a result, many North American, South American, and European companies are functioning more organically today. The process creates a new organization based on the best of the existing organization and shaped by what it wants to become. This new, optimal organization has seven essential competencies as part of its structure, which its members use in day-to-day operations:

1. Confidence
2. Commitment
3. Cocreation
4. Connection
5. Communication
6. Celebration (and course correction)
7. Crossing

Organic organizations need each competency to function organically. Figure 3 shows all seven competencies and how they interrelate:

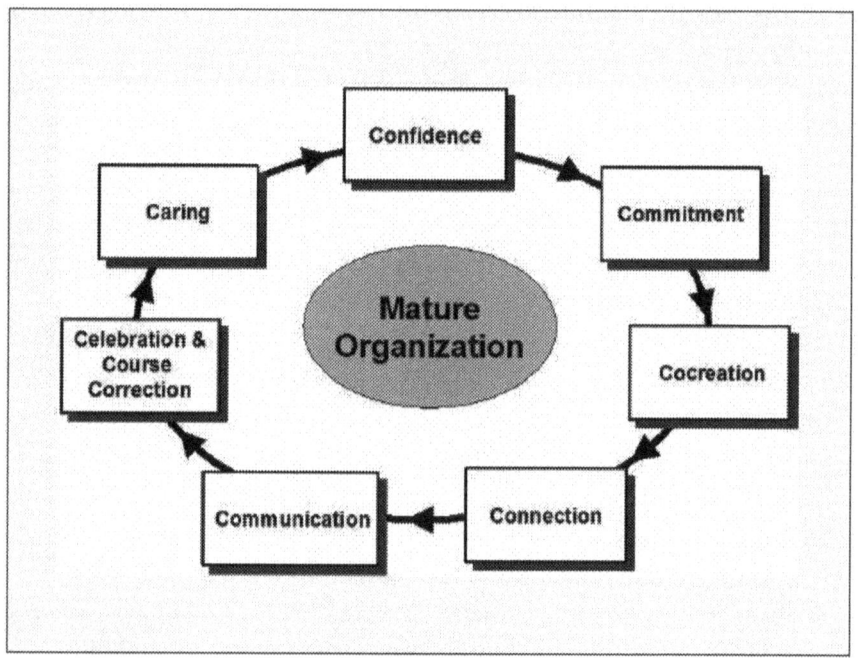

Figure 3: The seven Cs.

I will now briefly define each competency.

Confidence

The members of the organization believe that they can build the structures and the processes necessary to prosper and to reach their strategic objectives. They have the knowledge, abilities, and information that they need to transform these objectives into reality.

Commitment

The organization has clarity of purpose and its principles—the identity of the organization. The organization's members feel deeply committed to converting this identity into day-to-day operations. The close correlation between the identity of the individuals and the identity of the organization only deepens their dedication.

Cocreation

Everyone in the organization, at every level, is involved in creating its future. Together, they have developed a clear, positive, inspiring, and compelling vision of the future—shared by all—that clearly depicts the organization as it wants to be in five or ten years.

Connection

The desire to achieve the vision is powerful (I call this *future pull*). The organization clearly understands the difference between where it is today (the current reality) and where it needs to be to achieve its vision of the future. Thus, they know precisely what steps they must take to achieve it, and in what order. They are designing the processes and the structures that will achieve the strategic vision. The members of the organization are developing the muscles (knowledge, abilities, and information) they need to make the vision a reality. They are managing the organization through the vision rather than through a *power hierarchy*, that is, a system that is based on someone rising to the top—dominating others—through personal power of one sort or another. They manage the day-to-day business while building the ideal future organization.

Communication

An open environment exists where the members of the organization can communicate by means of many useful media. Communication is pleasant because the tools are easy to use, and information is available quickly and efficiently (high-tech and high-touch). It is easy for people to make good decisions with so much high-quality information available. Everyone gets frequent updates about their overall progress towards the strategic vision. The communication systems efficiently help manage the commitment to the vision throughout the organization.

Celebration and Course Correction

The organization confirms and adjusts its course, celebrating successes (achievements that move it closer to the strategic vision) and correcting any efforts that are not successful (not moving it toward the vision). It learns from its successes and failures.

Caring

The organization has created a climate of respect and confidence in its members—for themselves, their colleagues, shareholders, customers, and suppliers. Significant money and effort go toward adding value to the human capital of the organization and strengthening the relationships between stakeholders.

I am proposing that organizations worldwide take on a new sense of responsibility. Successful day-to-day function will no longer be enough. Administration, leadership, and management must constantly and strategically strive to move the organization to higher levels of maturity, through personal development and new, more mature organizational structures.

Results

For individuals, Organizational Architecture results in more confidence and higher self-esteem through successfully applying new "muscles" to circumstances that are increasingly challenging and complex. They experience heightened mutual respect for the other members of the organization and stakeholders, who increasingly respect them in return. Each employee is therefore more efficient and more valuable to the organization.

The organization, on the other hand, learns to manage more organically and productively inside a new and more profitable model of human relationships in the corporative environment. A mature, organic, and integrated structure is more agile, robust, and competitive.

Organizations are microcosms of society. Mature organizations produce more conscientious, ethical, and responsible individuals who invariably reshape the society in which they live.

The Organization's Choice

The leaders of the new millennium have a choice: They can continue extracting more results from systems in crisis, or ensure the creation of a more mature organization. The former guarantees obsolescence and failure, the latter guarantees success, economic survivability, and increased contribution to society.

Often, company directors and society leaders have this system of values at the core of their personal belief structures. Thus, resistance to change can be great. Many of these leaders came to their position of power by climbing the power hierarchy (often on the backs of others). They believe that substituting an organic values system for the hierarchical one would invalidate their entire career in one stroke. In fact, whereas power hierarchies cause so many problems, hierarchies based on function and ability are necessary for the effective profitability of any organization.

After the riot in Curaçao, I felt the need to help others to reevaluate the hierarchical values that had once seemed so natural—the values I had once seen as the basis for progress itself. Hierarchical thinking prevents human beings and their organizations from ever developing their true potential.

Every culture based on a rigid system of hierarchical values presumes there are people who are above, more capable, and better than those deemed below, less capable, and worse. This self-reinforcing belief system controls all human relations. It tells us there are superior and inferior people, leaders and followers, the chosen and the excluded. It justifies a rigid bureaucracy where orders come from above to control what and how it is below.

All levels of society accept this is as natural, as they do any widespread ideology. It produces deadwood, reduces motivation, and creates much anger and frustration among those disenfranchised by it. Its eventual result is a significant drop in interest and loss of motivation among all those that are at the bottom of the heap.

The same occurs in societies, on a macro scale. The populace, conditioned to rigid nonparticipative power hierarchies (haves versus have-nots, First World versus Third World), suffers from discontent and dissatisfaction, which, with day-to-day hardships, can well ignite uncontrolled explosions of anger and hostility. I am not a specialist in economics or politics. However, the global news media give evidence of this happening almost daily. It now has become the object of studies by economists, sociologists, anthropologists, social psychologists, corporate psychologists, and political theorists.

Financial capitalization on a global scale and the breakdown of the split between Western and Eastern Europe increasingly drove the center of power into the hands of corporations. This also occurred in Curaçao, where a few companies molded the entire society.

Back in the 1980s, I alerted my clients (North American, European, and Brazilian corporate leaders) that the world climate was becoming one that cultivates destructive emotional explosions and uncontrollable social tsunamis. Such upheavals will continue unless a substitute is found for the rigid hierarchical values structure prevalent in societies and organizations worldwide.

Today, we see an eerie similarity between the tsunami in Curaçao back in 1969 and the worldwide reactions following the terrorist attacks on September 11, 2001. The hierarchical values system used throughout the world is once again causing frustration and anger, this time at a global level (First World versus Third World). Satellite television and the Internet are making this obvious.

At first, I did not understand why people in many countries of the world rejoiced at the brutal and terrible events in New York on that day. Yet, when one looks at this tragic event from a structural perspective, the answer is simple. Hierarchy has once more created a painfully destructive state of affairs. For the deprived masses of the Third World, the United States is the most visible and convenient example of the First World, and so becomes the target for their anger.

To end this unrest, we must end hierarchy. We cannot do this by mandate or fiat, but only by reinventing the ways people, markets, and nations cooperate and do business. We must change the system of values that controls behavior at a personal, managerial, and social level. Otherwise, we shall continue to be subject to explosions of fury and aggression, public and private, threatening our organizations and indeed our civilization.

George Land, author and member of the New York Academy of Sciences, affirms that Western civilization is at a breakpoint. Land calls for radical cultural reinvention. I believe the event that we will always refer to as "9/11" has created a new baseline for present-day human conscience. We now have (or should have) a sense of duty to end global "hierarchicalism" by promoting the rapid maturing of individuals, companies, and societies. We need to produce more creative and profitable forms of production, management, and consumption. It is time for us to show heightened respect for one another and improve business processes among us. Only in this way will we forever drive out the specter of 9/11.

I sincerely believe that we can accelerate this process by setting up productive, participative, organic organizations. Companies reflect society, but they also influence it. For example, the communication industry is in the private sector, with its ability to spread cultural values and strongly influence behavior. If this industry were organic, however, it will soon spread this characteristic outwards into society, helping everyone to benefit from the ability to sail tidal waves.

One must believe that democracy is essential for the survival of organizations and the human race itself. To achieve this, we will have to regain confidence, show vigorous commitment, learn to cocreate our desired future and then to connect it to our current reality, improve our communication abilities, then celebrate each collective success together, and correct our course easily and naturally. We will then increasingly include caring in everything we do in our lives.

We must create conditions for a new business model that is more honest, productive, profitable, and just. We must gradually introduce and support this model in society, starting with companies. We will avoid the silent, destructive surge of an uncontrollable, frustrated, angry, and violent population, wherever it occurs.

I will talk about architecture of healthy organizations (and therefore societies) in this book. We can achieve the dreams of humanity through business. As I have expressed in the past[3], we are living in times that offer us great opportunities for reinvention, while obliging us to transform our world. These are times in which we will see the collapse of long-lived, closed systems and the rise of new democracies; times of intensified concern for ethics, compared to the past decades of opportunism and individualism; times in which ideas about relationships between individuals and the community—even the survival of our planet—are changing.

However, this book does not intend to address these broader issues directly. It will focus on the outcomes organizations can expect by seizing opportunities for transformation. Organizational Architecture recognizes that a more organic and mature business organization is essential. Only in this way can we achieve the creativity and agility necessary for sustainable progress in a world of constant transformation, where everything happens on a global scale and in real time. This will allow each of us in our own way to take part in building a worthwhile future.

---

3. Taken from an essay I wrote together with my Brazilian partner, Francisco Loschiavo Neto, for the book called *The Butterfly and the Dragon*, edited in 2000 by Axis Mundi with support from Instituto Ethos.

Chapter 2

Organic Transformation and Participative Management

The business world is experiencing rapid change because of abrupt and fundamental shifts in human and organizational behavior. This change has created many difficult challenges for managers in all business sectors all over the world.

With a few exceptions, the business models that corporations are using to manage processes and personnel date from the Industrial Revolution, when Western nations were inventing mass-production techniques. In that era, thinking was elitist and hierarchical, and this shaped the management models of the day. Following each market change, technological advance, or worldwide trend in management technique, business managers have given face-lifts to these models, using such tools as downsizing, *keiretsu*, re-reengineering, Total Quality Management, and empowerment. However, they have not changed the fundamentally hierarchical structure of the models.

These Industrial Age business models have become obsolete, although the business world is apparently ignorant of this fact. These models, in all fairness, brought us to where we are today. Because in the past they have proven to be successful, we continue to use them out of habit or tradition. In an environment where we have learned continuous processes improvement and refinement, we repeatedly, exhaustively, and foolishly try to improve on processes and fundamentally obsolete structures. Worst of all, we do this despite the knowledge that our organizations' performance is becoming progressively less profitable, and our management increasingly less effective!

The world is no longer the same as it was in the past. The business environment used to change in only marginal ways, and at a gradual pace. Limited responses to change, such as improvements to existing processes, were sufficient. Recently, however, the entire universe of production and consumption has changed so significantly that mere process refinement is not enough to thrive or even succeed. We must *reinvent* ways of working, producing, living, and doing business together!

In this new era, financial capital moves on a planetary scale. Technology has become commodity, and competition is likely to pop up anywhere. The growing availability of information at every level compels companies to be more alert and respond more quickly to the changing needs of their stakeholders (shareholders, employees, customers, suppliers, and community). It all demands a different organizational structure.

We need to re-create our business processes, systems, and management models to adapt to the new world that embraces us all, yet threatens our businesses with extinction. This must happen before our companies fall victim to the tsunamis caused by masses of people (including employees) that quietly but powerfully demand greater responsiveness to their needs, opportunities for participation, and personal growth.

Changes are forcing us to transform our organizations by recreating them. This must happen as we disassemble the current structure, opening the way for a radically different structure based on the previous one. With a new structure, based on new belief systems, we will be able to respond continuously, rapidly, and productively to the management challenges posed by this new world.

The structure of a house shapes and supports the behavior of the people who live in it. In organizations, as in any complex system, this is also true. For an organization to remain agile, productive, adaptable, resilient, and self-sustaining, the structure must continually change in response to the organization's needs. In other words, the structure of a complex system is nothing more than its response to the current needs that control its behavior. The structure must be able to adapt quickly to change, regardless of whether the changes are planned, spontaneous, or imposed.

In the past, companies could focus on their own production and business processes, forcing the market to adapt to their business model. Moreover, there was a time when management processes, systems, and models could afford to be elitist and hierarchical, organized from the top down. The subordinate internal levels and business units had to adapt themselves to the organization's centralized decisions. Organizations built, maintained, and vigorously defended internal and external boundaries, just as many companies (and countries) still do. They reinforced the rigid, elitist hierarchy at all levels as a defense against enemies. Unfortunately, the enemies that they were defending against were too often internal advocates trying to adapt the company to the changing needs of the marketplace.

Many companies continue to act in this way, despite paying a high price for their aging structures: declining profitability and poor long-term chances for survival. Symptoms include the inability to adapt, sluggish response to change, and dwindling productivity.

Globalization, relentless and irresistible since the middle of the twentieth century, is tearing down the barriers among nations. It is forcing companies to remove internal and external obstacles to trade. This has turned the world, as we know it, upside down. It has changed the way we live together and the way we produce, manage, and do business.

At the same time, competition has become hotter, simply because the marketplace has become the entire world—and instantaneous. The Internet, electronic cash transfers, and global couriers all threaten traditional sales and distribution. Customers (whether individuals or organizations) can now easily research, price, negotiate for, and buy almost anything from their computer in their own home or office. This is transforming business worldwide—in all sectors, segments, and markets.

Society and the market are experiencing deep-seated changes. They are becoming increasingly complex. Shareholders, employees, customers, suppliers, and the community (stakeholders) increasingly bring pressure upon companies to have greater agility and performance. They demand improved products, better results, and larger profits in an increasingly rapid cycle. In this environment, an already old-fashioned company will quickly decline. Just as in the ocean a shark will attack and eat a weakened prey, in business a better-organized and more agile company will "kill and eat" a moribund organization...or simply kill it, then gobble up that slice of the market.

To survive, companies must transform themselves into agile and responsive organisms, with the stamina of an adolescent and the abilities of a mature adult. They must discard the elitist hierarchy, undoing the myth that it is natural for all organizations to have superiors and inferiors. They must build a new organizational sailboat that allows them to sail through tsunamis.

Managing with Commitment

A company's most important asset is its stakeholders. Their commitment to the organization is crucial to its success. It must therefore understand, safeguard, and value their interests.

Historically, people have not been as valuable to a company as they are becoming today. Since the Industrial Revolution (indeed, as far back as the Agricultural Revolution) money or real capital has been the most essential asset that a company could have. In the Agricultural Era, for example, land was capital and made possible all production and commerce. In an Industrial Age factory, equipment was capital and was far more important than were its operators. You could always find or train someone to run a lathe, for example, but without the very expensive machine, there could be no product or production and therefore no factory.

Recently, the changes brought about by the Information Revolution have reduced the importance of real capital. Almost anyone is able to buy a computer and a broadband Internet connection, for instance, and do real work from his or her home-office. This reduces the value of the company's physical capital with respect to individual's knowledge and his or her ability to use it effectively. Thus, capital is shifting from the traditional capitalist and corporation to the individual worker and the intellectual tools that he or she owns. The change from valuing people based on how well they serve the capital equipment to valuing them for their own capital—what they know and what they can do—increasingly describes the modern world.

As I said earlier, there was a time when power was in the hands of those who owned land. Then the Industrial Revolution transferred power to those who owned machinery and tools. With the coming of the Information Age and the Internet, power has begun the shift to those who have the knowledge and who know how to transform it into competitive advantage and lasting profits.

Attracting and keeping these skilled *knowledge workers* requires a different strategy. Traditionally, wage increases based on tenure with the company were enough to keep a skilled worker for his or her entire career. This is no longer the case. Companies that cling to these practices are losing assets, talent, and competitiveness at an ever-increasing pace. Knowledge workers must have useful opportunities for self-improvement, or else they will become frustrated to the point of feeling anger and resentment, and simply find somewhere else to work.

Knowledge workers also demand respect and recognition for what they know, rather than their position in the hierarchy. Because elitist, hierarchical values systems and their outdated methods still prevail in most organizations today, the number of disgruntled professionals is increasing as companies refuse to recognize or use appropriately the talents and professional experience of these men and women.

In order to rid themselves of their hierarchical elitism, organizations must go through structural transformation to set up a system of organic values. This type of transformation increases the company's ability to innovate, integrate, and respond. At the same time, it strengthens the commitment between the internal stakeholders and the organization by recognizing and promoting talent. It expands the organization's productivity, increases profitability, and enhances its ability to survive in an increasingly hostile and tsunami-filled world.

In other words, the organization must transform itself to meet the challenges of the new environment. The transformation must revitalize the organization while catering to the needs of all stakeholders. It must enable every stakeholder to act in an organic way. It must ensure that all efforts satisfy the company's purpose (based on its identity and values) and the needs of its stakeholders (especially its customers). This is the only way to ensure that organizations survive internal and external tsunamis.

Before continuing, let me clarify the terms *purpose*, *values*, and *identity*. The popular press has sometimes used these words improperly, and I want to make sure that the reader understands their true meaning.

Purpose is the organization's reason for existence. We cannot express this quantitatively or within a specific period, because purpose is the reason behind an organization's existence. We always connect purpose to specific customers' needs, whether individuals or organizations. This implies that purpose can change as customer needs and business processes change.

Values are the set of basic principles or guiding beliefs that allow an organization to align with its purpose and shape the way that it achieves its purpose. Values separate an organization is from what it is not. They are the rules that the organization plays by. They are the organization's specific beliefs that guide its behavior and all decisions. An organization would only alter its values to adapt to significant environmental changes.

Finally, *identity* is the organization's demonstration of internal and external attitudes as it pursues its purpose. One can best see a company's identity in the way it interacts with its stakeholders, rather than the image portrayed by its advertising. To use a popular cliche, the organization reveals its identity in the way it walks the walk, as opposed to the way it talks the talk. The identity may change because of adjustments to its values or redirection of its purpose.

Organizations reach maturity when there is a high degree of integration between values, purpose, and identity. The shareholders and employees are in alignment with the purpose and are willing to do what it takes to achieve it.

An Integrated and Productive Organism

Emotional well-being is a fundamentally important characteristic of productivity. It is as important as capital, technology, tools, and raw materials. Emotional well-being expands people's productive capacity by making them receptive to innovation. It strengthens their interest in and their awareness of what they do, and boosts their reasoning and understanding. It increases their yearning for achievement. Although traditional management training rarely stresses it, and even though the concept is new to the business environment, people need happiness and contentment in the workplace just as much as they do in everyday life.

Healthy organisms depend on a realistic approach toward the environment, as well as suitable internal conditions, for survival, growth, and reproduction. Organic companies have a continuous awareness of their environment, no matter how far-reaching, and have realistic attitudes toward it. Organic growth is a process of continuously satisfying needs through contact with the environment.

Of all organisms, only humans are able to act strategically, to use a vision of a possible future to guide its behavior. Only humans try to transcend the limits of their environment to reach a preferred state. The Hindu writing *Brihadaranyaka Upanishad* says, "the depth of your being dictates your desire; your desire dictates your will; your will dictates your acts; your acts dictate your destiny." Human organizations share this desire.

The New Business Model

We can describe the new business model as follows:

The strategy and tactics necessary to reach the proposed objectives contained in a desired future, as projected and set forth in a corporate vision; based on a sincere understanding of the organization's identity, the values that define its culture, and the environmental factors to which it is subject, all aligned with its noble purpose.

Thus, I close the cycle, the reason behind this book.

In today's world, and from now on, companies must use a system of organic values that coherently composes the company's identity as it strives to reach its purpose. Such an organic organization will have the ability to:

- Propose its own strategic objectives, drawn from a clear understanding of its values, needs, and environmental conditions.

- Retain individual talents and strengthen them to the utmost.

- Commit its shareholders and employees to a single shared global strategic objective, expressed in a corporative vision arising from the company's purpose and values, toward which it directs all activity.

- Define the best possible choices among all those that exist.

- Quickly adapt to each new external or internal environmental change.

- Experience healthy reinforcement and expand its capacity for agility, surviving and competing in an atmosphere of well-being.

This new organic system will naturally spread out to society in general, and will infuse a more agile, innovative, adaptive, and integrated way of living and interacting together. It will reduce the tsunami-producing tension once caused by the rigid, unproductive, controlling, and elitist hierarchy that it replaces.

Chapter 3

A New Company for a New Consciousness

The changes mentioned in the previous chapter have resulted in a fundamental transformation in the collective human consciousness. Our expectations have changed for production, consumption, affection, and social relationships, as well as the way that we set up partnerships (at business or family levels). Its effects are visible all over the world.

This evolution transcends national and cultural boundaries. People and companies are experiencing such rapid paradigm shifts that people's needs and the offerings designed to meet those needs are changing at a rate unprecedented in human history.

This has produced a level of creative tension in the world that, when released, will generate a tsunami of unprecedented size and power. This giant wave will inevitably crash against the rigid hierarchical structures of our societies and organizations. If we, as individuals, organizations, or societies, are to survive this cataclysm, we will need to anticipate it and take effective action. We need to put into place more resilient, agile, and responsive social and organizational models that will help us sail the oncoming tidal wave.

We must set new expectations for organizational behavior. It must be essentially different—not just cosmetic. What I am proposing for organizations is similar to psychotherapy that restructures someone's personal life. This therapy is more than just working on a limited group of issues an individual believes to be causing problems in life. Rather, it deals with the entire set of guiding beliefs (knowledge, qualities, and attitudes) that direct a person's day-to-day actions.

The Rise of a New Consciousness

Significant advances in the human race's consciousness level have always resulted from new technologies that give people more control over their environment. Fire, agriculture, the wheel, gunpowder, electricity, internal combustion, and the Internet are some examples. However, few people can predict how a new technology will change the way that people view the world and deal with it from that point forward.

Changing levels of consciousness create different personal and societal needs and motivations, as Abraham Maslow showed in his *Hierarchy of Needs* model (Maslow, 1954). The needs of the consumer drive the marketplace, so organizations must continually reinvent themselves to respond effectively to those changing needs. Organizations that are not aware of these changes cannot reinvent themselves. They appear unresponsive, and quickly lose the loyalty of their stakeholders.

Many experts consider loyalty to be one of a company's most important assets. Customers often buy out of brand loyalty. A company that loses customer loyalty not only loses sales, but it often stops being loyal to the customer, which further reduces customer loyalty. This destructive spiral wrecks revenues, talents, market share, and brand equity.

It is sadly interesting to list the corporations that forged the technology that is changing our consciousness worldwide, and to note how many have failed. They overinvested in an obsolete way of doing business and were unable to respond to the motivations and needs that they themselves produced. Thus, they become victims of tsunamis that they created.

Companies in general have a poor awareness of changes in the marketplace, so they continually invest in programs for perfecting methods and processes without considering the undeniable change in human consciousness. As they try to perfect the ways that they have always done business, they grind themselves down by repeatedly improving fundamentally obsolete processes.

They do not understand the transformations in human consciousness that globalization has produced. Neither do they understand transculturalization caused by the Internet nor the extent of this change. They continue to be unaware that choosing quantity over quality and duplication over innovation will inevitably lead companies to decline and societies to destruction. They lack the ability to invent the more effective model to deal with the new forms of production, business, and management that they need. As a result, they increasingly fail to satisfy the needs of their stakeholders. This creates dissatisfaction and resentment in the stakeholders and results in poor productivity.

The worldwide economy has experienced astounding growth over the last decade, due largely to the success of many of the world's leading companies. However, in many cases, the methods that they have chosen to bring about this improved performance will eventually cause their downfall in a boomerang effect. Just look at some of the companies in Hong Kong, Korea, Indonesia, and Japan whose recent decline clearly proves this argument. All four of these countries have experienced remarkable economic expansion, followed by serious productive and market crises. Their boom in the 1980s and their collapse in the 1990s is the direct result of their myopic devotion to process improvement. It is true that for a short time these companies became more efficient. This resulted in good returns for investors, both in dividends and increased share value. However, the benefits of these improvement efforts proved temporary, and the companies declined as fast as they had risen. These organizations traded their regenerative capacity for self-absorbed process improvement and gave up their agility in pursuit of higher profits. The tsunami swept them away.

Radical Changes to the Human Ego

Alvin Toffler, in his book *Future Shock* (1970) introduced and popularized the term *wave* when applied to changing societal and technological trends. A giant tidal wave now threatens our business and social life, and there is nothing to do but try to survive by learning how to sail it.

Humanity, in its natural desire to become a creator of its destiny has developed technology, such as the computer, that allows it to be almost omnipresent and omniscient. Technology has unexpectedly become a tool for developing the human ego and has taken us to new levels of conscience and needs, in an unprecedented and all-embracing advance.

Even so, many business leaders and organizations see this trend as simply a continuation of the Industrial Revolution. This is not the case! The Industrial Revolution forced organizations with structures left over from the Agricultural Era to transform or die. Two centuries ago, the world's economic, political, and cultural map changed, and the range of humanity's behavioral needs and possibilities expanded sharply. The Information Revolution swept away many of the remaining social and business practices of the Industrial Age; the latest tsunami that I am calling the Virtuality Revolution is sweeping away the rest.

Many indicators tell us that this is happening. The Industrial Revolution, for example, gave a tremendous boost to companies that could effectively address the new opportunities, market pressures, and the changes in business processes. It stifled companies that could not adapt (or would not), causing them to disappear.

Information technology is doing much more than creating new production, consumption, and business processes. It is making those processes more practicable and profitable. It is changing the very framework within which it is happening. Before information technology began transforming the planet, people took hierarchical values for granted. Some people in the organization were simply considered better because of their rank or level. The shift in awareness caused by information technology has shown concepts of superior and inferior to be myths. Lately, as I said before, organizations have begun to value people more for their ability than for their position.

The Virtuality Revolution has intensified this change. Instantaneous, global communication via the Internet has widely dispersed these changes in consciousness by ignoring geographic barriers. Before instant communication, changes to the social and business processes could take place at significantly different rates in different regions of the globe. Today, a change in one region is broadcast everywhere within minutes of its happening. Ideas, trends, and beliefs travel throughout the world regardless of language or culture.

Information technology is bringing about a different world. To survive and be successful in this new world, organizations must quickly become more resilient, agile, and mature. They must develop attitudes, strategies, and structures that are qualitatively different from those that have so far prevailed.

Stages of Ego Development

As mentioned in Chapter 1, my colleagues and I studied Jane Loevinger's work on the Stages of Ego Development during our research in Curaçao, which began shortly after the May 1969 events. We think of the Ego Stages as phases of emotional maturity. In the early 1970s, at Washington University in St. Louis, Dr. Loevinger showed that the human ego matures sequentially in identifiable stages (Loevinger, 1970). Part of a spectrum that ranges from immaturity to maturity, each stage is independent of chronological age and is identified by the manner in which people see and deal with the world.

Loevinger's stages are not absolutes. They do not have sharply defined boundaries that a person is either inside or outside of. It is, however, easy to identify a person's predominant ego stage. At each stage, he or she has different expectations, attitudes, and degrees of commitment to him- or herself, to productive endeavor, to organizations, and to life in general. A person's level of maturity is therefore the result of the opportunities that he or she has had to progress through naturally from one stage to the next. This progress occurs as people satisfy increasingly complex personal needs, such as physical survival, safety, social acceptance, or self-realization (Maslow, 1954).

Each ego stage has an associated cognitive style, process style, and systemic style. The cognitive style is how they reason and make sense of a situation. The process style is how they express emotions and influence one another. The systemic style is how they function, cope with the world, and carry out survival tasks. In other words, people always sense the world and respond to it according to the ego development stage that matches most closely to their current psycho-emotional framework. They adopt specific attitudes about their actions, including their jobs, with differing abilities for fixing and upholding commitments.

Loevinger defined six distinct and successive ego development stages: *impulsive, self-protective, conformist, conscientious, autonomous,* and *integrated.* Each stage has four distinct behavioral dimensions: impulse control (or character development), interpersonal style, cognitive style, and conscious preoccupation. Table 3 shows each of these stages and explains the details of each behavioral dimension.

Table 3: Behavioral Characteristics According to Ego Development Stage

Dimension	Impulsive	Self-protective	Conformist
Impulse Control	Does not recognize rules. Sees action as bad only if punished. Impulsive. Afraid of retaliation. Has temper tantrums.	Recognizes rules but only obeys for immediate advantage. Has expedient morality. Action bad only if caught. Blames others, but does not see self as responsible for failure or trouble.	Partially internalizes rules; obeys without question. Feels shame for consequences. Concerned with shoulds. Morally condemns other's points of view. Denies sexual and aggressive feelings.

Dimension	Impulsive	Self-protective	Conformist
Interpersonal Style	Dependent and exploitative, unconscious dependence. Treats people as sources of supply.	Manipulative and exploitative. Wary and distrusting of others' intentions. Opportunist. Zero-sum. I win, you lose. Shameless, shows little remorse.	Wants to belong to group, to gain social acceptance. Feels mutual trust within a group, prejudice against other groups. Socially agreeable although with superficial pleas-antness. Likes offering help to oth-ers. Understands relationships in terms of actions rather than feel-ings or motives.
Cognitive Style	Thinks in a dichot-omous way. Has simple, global ideas. Conceptu-ally confused. Thinks concretely. Egocentric.	As at left.	Thinks stereotypi-cally. Uses clichés. Sees in terms of superlatives. Has a sentimental men-tality. Has little introspection: refer-ence to feelings ordinary or stereo-typed.
Conscious Preoccupation	Sex and aggres-sion. Is obsessed with bodily func-tions.	Self-protection to gain control and advantage. Wants to dominate and fears domination, being controlled or deceived by oth-ers. Seeks to get the better of oth-ers, even by deceiving them.	Appearances. Social acceptance to group norms. Gives value to hier-archical systems, material posses-sions, status sym-bols, reputation, and prestige.

Dimension	Conscientious	Autonomous	Integrated
Impulse Control	Self-assessment according to existing standards. Self-critical with tendency to be hypercritical. Feels guilty for consequences.	Concerned with moral principles. Tolerates multiplicity of viewpoints. Concerned with conflicting duties, roles, and principles.	Reconciles internal conflicts and external conflicting demands. Concerned with justice. Is creative and spontaneous.
Interpersonal Style	Has sense of responsibility, obligation. Has mutually intensive relationships. Concerned with communication and expression of differentiated sentiments.	Wants autonomy in relations. Sees relations as involving situations of unavoidable interdependence. Tolerates other's solutions of conflicts. Respects others' autonomy. Is open.	Appreciates and stimulates individual differences.
Cognitive Style	Conceptually complex. Has a sense of consequences and priorities. Aware of contingencies, sees alternatives. Sees self in context of community, society.	Has greater conceptual complexity and tolerates ambiguity. Has capacity to see paradox, contradictions. Has broad scope of thought in time frame, social context. Perceives human interdependence and is very objective.	Has sense of self as part of flow of human condition.

Dimension	Conscientious	Autonomous	Integrated
Conscious Preoccupation	Achievement of long-term goals. Motivation, reasons for behavior. Self-identification with feelings, personal traits.	Individuality and self-fulfillment. Conflicting inner needs. Nonhostile, existential humor.	Integrated sense of unique identity. Sees life as interconnected whole.

Note that in this book I have substituted the term *opportunistic* for the term *self-protective* when describing that ego stage. I have found that this is an equivalent term and better suits our requirements.

Table 3 helps to explain why there is such a close relationship between someone's maturity level and his or her quality of life, as well as his or her performance within the organization. Both increase at higher stages of ego maturity. The individual's ego maturity stage predicts his or her behavior, and characterizes that individual's performance possibilities within the organization. For instance, attitudes such as "I will only do this if I earn more for it" or "I will only do it if I am told to" are typical of the impulsive and opportunistic stages of maturity, respectively. The more mature attitudes, "I will only do what they expect me to" or "I will only do what is best for the organization," are characteristic of the conformist and conscientious stages. The following story illustrates individual motivation at different stages of ego development:

> Centuries ago, a great cathedral was being built at the top of a hill. A curious friar, watching the stonemasons work, wondered what motivated them to do their job. He approached three of them and asked them why they were working on the project. The first said, "I make money by hauling stone on my shoulders, and this is how I survive." The second said, "I work here because my family has always been masons and they expect it of me." The third said, "I do this because all my life I have wanted to help build a great cathedral, and this work fulfills my dream!"

All of them probably wanted their gravestone to read, "He worked hard, and did it well." Yet, each man's individual motivation was different. The first was driven by personal survival needs, and the second by the expectations of others. The third was self-actualized; we can easily guess which one was more motivated to do excellent work.

Loevinger helps us to understand how individuals mature. She also reminds us that the motivation to become more mature results from stimulation in the deepest and most private parts of a person's personality. Before the ego can move on to the next higher stage, becoming more mature, certain personal needs at each stage must be satisfied. We must remember, too, that the organizational culture has a very strong influence on those that work within it. An individual cannot mature unless all three cultures—personal, professional, and social—support the new maturity level.

The current worldwide business culture is essentially mechanistic, hierarchical, and undemocratic (or even antidemocracy and thus totalitarian). Unfortunately, people performing at the higher levels of individual maturity need an organizational climate that supports organic and interdependent (mature) behavior. Only by creating this type of business culture can organizations minimize unproductive behavior, or prevent the convulsions that cause tsunamis.

To begin thinking about creating new business cultures, it is important to understand more about the possibilities. Roger Harrison's work on cultural models within organizations (1972) shows the existence of four distinct organizational ideologies, as follows:

1. *Power oriented*—tries to dominate the environment and overcome all and any opposition, refusing to give in to any external force, practicing absolute control over its subordinates.

2. *Role oriented*—tries to be as rational and well-ordered as possible. In contrast to the autocracy of a power-oriented organization, he or she is concerned about legitimacy, legality, and responsibility, which are valued to the same extent as competence. In general, this type admires the correct answer more than an efficient answer, and changes slowly.

3. *Task oriented*—values fulfilling far-reaching objectives. Everyone must carry out their tasks, and great emphasis is placed on agility and prompt reaction to changes that arise.

4. *Individual oriented*—exists mainly to fulfill the needs of its members. Expects people to influence one another through example, inclination to help, and caring, and prefers consensus-based decision methods.

We know that mature workers need an organic and participative work structure, but what would such a structure look like? By combining Harrison's description of the task-oriented structure and his individual-oriented structure, we gain a clearer picture of such an organization.

The next step then becomes understanding how to achieve this organization. Harvard Professor David C. McClelland's work, *The Achievement Motive* (1953), gave us a recipe for a more mature, dynamic worker. According to McClelland, there are three possible main motives that drive a person's general behavior: power, affiliation, or accomplishment. The individual's behaviors and objectives come directly from the strongest motive.

- People with *power motivation* are interested chiefly in controlling others, in the search to satisfy their needs;

- People with *affiliation motivation* seek to preserve good relations with others above all, to develop intimacy and harmony within the group;

- People with *achievement motivation* give priority to carrying out tasks, in a search for professional excellence and rational solution of problems.

McClelland found that when individuals are achievement-motivated, they are more productive and valuable to their organization. When achievement motivates an entire society, it thrives socioeconomically. Affiliation- and (especially) power-motivated societies fail. Therefore, we saw the need to build a society and business organizations filled with achievement-motivated individuals.

Armed with this newfound knowledge about maturity, organizational structures, and individual motivation, my colleagues and I set out to discover the solution for social inequality. We had the rare opportunity of having at our disposal an ideal microcosm in which to experiment: an entire country! Curaçao has a population of only 150,000 people and is the center of a wide variety of commercial enterprises. In addition, we had the support of all the local business and political leaders. We were able to experiment with different methods for changing the business structures, working within distinct social strata and different functional levels inside different organizations.

By the early 1970s, I was already working closely with Dr. Harry Lasker, one of the principal McClelland collaborators, who had decided to remain in Willemstad, Curaçao's capital city. He wanted to research the similarity between the research carried out in Curaçao and previous results he had seen in India, where he and McClelland had done individual and organizational development projects.

In our search for behavioral standards, we surveyed more than five thousand people, correlating Loevinger's, McClelland's, and Rotter's methods, as I mentioned before (Lasker, 1972). During the 1970s and 1980s, we were able to develop and apply several change programs intended to help the population advance to more mature stages of ego development (Lasker, 1977).

Over the years we continued to work within these three conceptual frameworks and added "predominant organizational ideology" (Harrison, 1972, 119–128). Further research showed a high degree of correlation between Harrison's work and the other three. We were able to create an integrated approach that applied all four theories to organizational change. This method later became Organizational Architecture. We were able to confirm its efficacy through organizational development projects in different companies and countries all over the world.

We found that people who are motivated by power or affiliation motivation are normally at lower levels of maturity. They respond poorly to achievement motivation training. Only people with more developed intellectual skills, knowledge, and abilities and greater emotional maturity respond well. These individuals are able to manage the tension that exists between current conditions and the desired future. Achievement motivation always requires a high level of personal maturity.

Thus, it became ever clearer why many companies react poorly to change and (paradoxically) resist achievement. It is because companies generally consist of people in the opportunistic or conformist stages of ego development. Companies always depend on and reflect the ego maturity and motivational standards of their principal internal stakeholders. Many companies struggle against achievement because they have frozen into their founder's ideological standards. No matter how loud their promodernization talk or how much they invest in organizational development programs, they do not have the collective maturity to achieve lasting change.

Immaturity decreases productivity and profitability, increases pressure for immediate results, reduces confidence, and reinforces resistance to innovation and adaptation. It produces unconscious, fearful, and destructive resentment. This combination leads the company inevitably toward decline.

Resistance to Change

At the personal level, what decides resistance to change? Experienced and well-educated people have the ability to see the need for change when it arises. Why then do they uphold an elitist, hierarchical values system? Why do they insist on the status quo, even though it causes poor productivity and resentment from those held back in their careers? Why do they defend a system that produces so much anxiety and apprehension in those who have achieved (or inherited) lofty positions in the hierarchy?

Most people choose the company they work for because their personal values align with their view of the chosen company's values (whether they are conscious of this reasoning or not). They sincerely want the company to prosper, thus providing favorable opportunities for professional and personal development. If this is true, then how can we explain individuals' and organizations' intense resistance to change? Why do they fight to maintain the status quo on one hand, while admitting that they need to change in order to increase productivity, thus satisfying their own interests, on the other?

The studies in Curaçao suggest that the hierarchical values systems have led us all to believe that elitist hierarchies are inherent to life. Examples include the king or queen and his or her subjects, the owner and his or her employees, the director and his or her subordinates, the First World and the Third World. In an elitist hierarchy people at the top are constantly struggling not to fall, while those at the bottom are always striving to pull themselves up. No one is ever truly content. The rigidity of the hierarchical structure gives an illusion of safety, even though there is none.

Resistance to change at a collective level (in societies, organizations, and companies) usually comes from individual resistance. Concepts developed by Wilhelm Reich and Fritz Perls showed us how personal and group resistance to organizational change occurs.

German psychoanalyst Wilhelm Reich coined the term "Character Armor" in 1933 to describe psycho-emotional protective behavior. Reich showed that each time an individual feels incapable of satisfying a basic need or solving a crucial conflict, he or she adds habitual unconscious defenses against a specific emotion (Reich, 1933). A person keeps these defenses throughout life as character armor, incorporating them into his or her identity. Without clearly realizing it, yet compelled by the character armor, people create the exact circumstances from which they want to protect themselves. This justifies the existence of the armor, in a vicious and unending behavior cycle ("See why I have to act like that?").

Character armor starts in early in ego development (the impulsive stage). Quick anger in response to a perceived attack, or simply turning your back on an opponent, can be an effective defense when very young. Babies use it all the time to protect themselves from perceived threats. Such behavior, however, becomes tiresome and ineffective when the individual continues to use it by subconscious habit later in life. If, after having reached adulthood, the person's ego development has not moved past the impulsive stage, his or her world-view stagnates, and his or her general behavior becomes unproductive and poorly motivated. An impulsive person sees the world in a dichotomist and Manichean way: black versus white, good versus bad, or right versus wrong. His or her choices are limited to imposing his or her will or not—to do battle or not. He or she has no ability to become interdependent through adaptation and compromise.

People at the opportunistic stage give top priority to creating a safe world for themselves. People feel insecure but do not recognize this, and so project their own wants and fears on the external world, normally in a polarized and combative manner, shielding themselves behind previously tested and known rules.

By the time they reach the conformist stage, people have satisfied their primary needs for survival (in the impulsive stage) and personal safety (in the opportunistic stage). Their entire behavior is oriented toward acceptance and approval, even if this is not productive for that person or the group.

This process continues, with the character armor defining and limiting the personality, imposing ineffective behavior and reducing adaptability. Thus, the individual is set up for failure on contact with the environment. To be successful, an individual (or organization) must always have an agile connection between external stimulus and internal reality.

Organizational Character Armor

It is important for us to understand that any significant change in an organization or a society always causes strong resistance from all its members. A significant number of management modernization examples fail specifically by ignoring the effects of character armor. When they do not take into account the effects of human resistance to change, they will not produce the results that they promised to the organization.

People form character armor during infancy. In organizations, this happens during their early formation phase. Traumatic events happen in a particular stage of development, and the individuals in the company are unable to respond effectively so they develop rigidity in their attitudes. These rigid attitudes can threaten the organization's survival when it really needs to change. At the individual level, we often say, "Look at Joe doing the same thing again. Why doesn't he learn?" At the organizational level, we say, "If everyone knows that change is necessary, then why hasn't the company done it by now?" It cannot, because its character armor will not let it.

In Reichean therapy, practitioners manipulate specific muscle groups in order to release trapped feelings and emotions. The organizational architecture process manipulates the company's muscles (attitudes, beliefs, knowledge, and skills), freeing the organization from rigid, confining attitudes.

In organizations, we see character armor most often displayed as hierarchical behavior. The hierarchy keeps all internal stakeholders frozen in predefined roles. It guards against opportunities for personal development because this might give stakeholders the ambition and ability to rebel against the status quo. Organizations keep their hard-won character armor even when faced with the clear need to adapt. This causes loss of productivity, opportunities, assets, and talents.

Integrated Simultaneous Development

Social and business organizations desperately need a process that allows them to reinvent themselves by changing their basic motivations and by helping their internal stakeholders become more mature. Only this will cause the deep and lasting improvement in their ability to innovate what they need to win a sustainable increase in their overall productivity. And only this will overcome the hierarchical values system to which the less-mature ego stages cling.

At present, less mature egos dominate organizations. Their elitist, hierarchical values system imposes severe limits on what the organization can achieve. It reduces productivity and creates desperation among the stakeholders. Perhaps most importantly, the resentment that hierarchy causes within the lower functional or social levels can lead to an explosive search for alternatives—a tsunami like the one that washed over Curaçao in 1969.

The advance from one stage to another during organizational transformation projects involves weakening the company's organizational character armor. This happens through the direct participation of its shareholders and employees in creating an improved or optimal organization. As they accomplish change, internal stakeholders learn how to be successful in overcoming obstacles and resolving dilemmas. This helps them to mature and, therefore, respond more effectively to the needs of the customers, suppliers, and stockholders.

The changes that occur in the internal stakeholders do not remain within the boundaries of the organization, either. They improve people's lives outside the organization, too. Eventually their personal growth and maturity will shape their families, their community, and indeed their social environment in a mature and positive way.

In an organization, if top managers are at the first stages of ego development (which is common), they try to set up and preserve a business culture based on their personal style. This in turn attracts employees in similar ego development stages, which keeps the culture as it is, hindering creativity and change. Therefore, even if the current managers learn new management techniques, the organization will defend against them to keep its culture as is, reaffirming the old barriers. This explains why management transformation methods based only on perfecting existing practices prove ineffective over the long-term.

The process needs to make it easier for the company as a whole to advance to higher stages of maturity, both at a personal (internal stakeholders) and organizational (management practices) level. Shareholders and employees will feel more satisfied with their individual needs for survival, security, acceptance, self-affirmation, participation, personal growth, and creative autonomy as they advance to the higher stages of ego maturity.

The organizational intervention must be organic, tailored to each specific client, because every organization has specific and changing needs at every stage of development. The organization must be treated as a unified whole, as must each internal part, whether that part is a functional group, process, or individual stakeholder. Organically transforming an organization is much the same as giving birth to it all over again, except that this time you start with the best of what already exists. The organization must fully reinvent itself according to the needs of its stakeholders (all those with an interest in the company), based on its identity, its values, and its purpose. It must constantly scan the internal and external environment that defines its boundaries. It must regularly define and communicate short-, medium-, and long-term objectives. It must continuously adapt its internal business processes to these objectives in a cocreative way, resulting in more mature behavior within the company.

The organization must become an adaptable organism, responding competently to new market and economic challenges with organic agility. Although this will involve redefining its internal processes, it will extend to setting up production, business, and managerial relations with partners, who are no longer merely suppliers or vendors. In this way, it will become a profitable, self-sustaining, and confident organism.

Otherwise, as we have already seen, a lasting organizational transformation will remain only a dream.

Chapter 4

Integrating to Improve Profitability and Permanence

In the last chapter, I showed that to survive an organization must undergo transformation from hierarchy to organic organism. To ensure its long-term survival, an organic organization must develop certain specific essential competencies—skills, abilities, or areas of expertise—and constantly use them in all its actions or decisions. These competencies support an egalitarian, harmonious, and integrated values system. This values system affects the organizational structure (the hierarchy of functions, products, processes, and control systems), its internal stakeholders (employees, stockholders, and managers), the environment (the macroeconomic sector and business segments), and external stakeholders (customers, suppliers, and the community). Each competency adds value to the organization, and must therefore be recognized and rewarded. They help the company become alive, actively striving toward its own organic existence—an integrated whole.

The Seven Cs

There are seven specific essential competencies that an organic system needs for success. I call these seven essential competencies the Seven Cs. They reinforce the corporate purpose, identity, and values and support every effort to fulfill the company's vision and thus meet customer and stakeholder needs. The Seven Cs reduce the need to hire outsiders to provide necessary skills and knowledge. They affect its day-to-day existence in a positive, effective, efficient, and lasting way.

The Seven Cs are a set, comprehensive and indivisible. Each competency is important on its own but is linked to and interdependent with the other six. Although we can look at each competency individually, we must always consider them as a group. However, the speed at which the company develops each competency and its level in comparison with the other competencies may differ.

We can use the Seven Cs as a tool to bring about a living, sustainable organization that is complete and self-reinforcing. Such a company can integrate many different positions and points of view in a mature way, setting up a productive environment. Similarly, a company that effectively employs all Seven Cs does away with conditions such as neglect, oversight, or exclusion that result in tsunamis of sabotage or explosive outbursts of resentment among the ones the organization neglected, overlooked, or excluded.

As shown in Figure 4, each competency is an integral part of the set, and each interconnects in a way that strengthens the other six. Organizational Architecture helps the organization—and every individual within the organization—to fully develop each competency and to apply them to each decision and every circumstance.

The Seven Cs mutually and continuously reinforce one another. Confidence, for instance, increases commitment. Commitment supports cocreation in a connected and communicating way. Through effective communication, the organization knows when to celebrate successes and when to correct misdirected efforts. With the other Cs in place, the organization is able to be more caring for all levels of the organization and for its external stakeholders. In turn, this increases confidence and commitment, propelling the company in a continuous, rising spiral of ever-improving, healthy, organic behavior.

It is important to understand that although a healthy organization needs all Seven Cs, the sequence in which Organizational Architecture works with each depends on the organization's present condition (current reality) at the onset of each project.

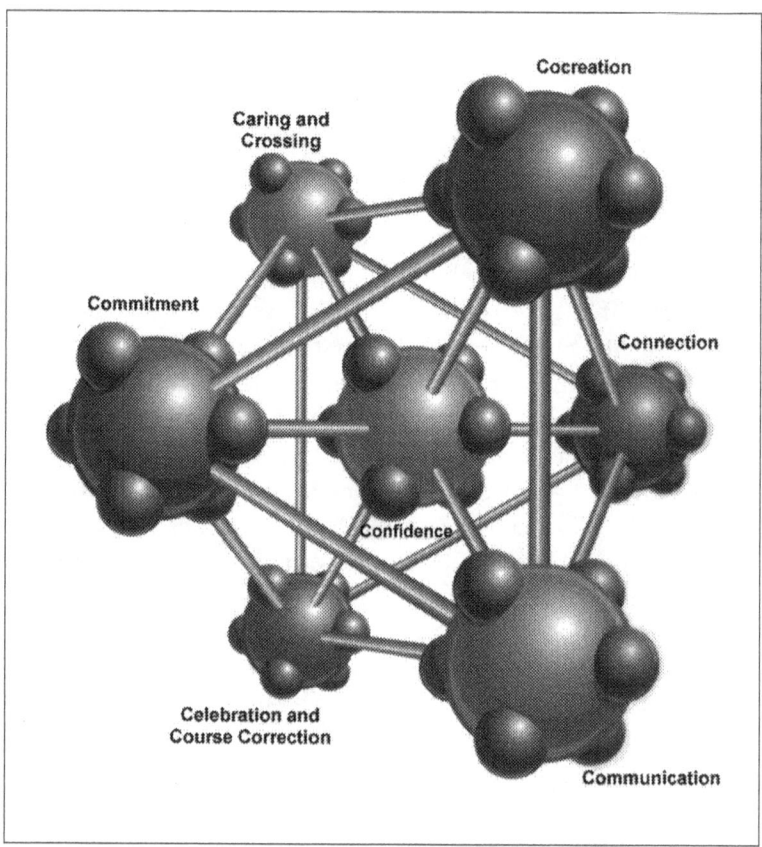

Figure 4: The Seven Cs essential to organic companies.

Before looking into the ways that these essential competencies bring their immeasurable benefits to an organization, let me briefly describe each one of them:

1. Confidence: The conviction that the members of the organization have the power to design, plan, and put in place (or build) a new organization. It is the certainty that it will successfully meet the challenges of the future, because it has, through its members, the knowledge, skill, and information that it needs.

2. Commitment: An organization-wide dedication to carrying out the purpose, bringing it to life in day-to-day action, giving the organization a reason for existence based on the specific needs and demands

of its internal and external stakeholders. Another important characteristic of commitment is organization-wide rededication to the shared values or guiding beliefs that will continuously guide all actions to fulfill these needs and demands.

3. Cocreation: All stakeholders set a global direction for the company through collective deliberation and consensus. The result of cocreation is that the organization continually renews the corporate vision, taking into consideration changes in its environment. This allows it to build in the present what it wants to be in the future.

4. Connection: The practice of linking the corporate vision to the company's current reality. This allows the organization to define, orchestrate, and carry out the steps that it must take to convert today's vision into tomorrow's reality.

5. Communication: The knowledge interconnection among internal stakeholders (shareholders and employees). This keeps them focused on and aligned with the vision by making them aware of the progress of the organizational transformation at every stage, now and in the future.

6. Celebration and Course Correction: Praising results that move the organization toward the vision (successes) and redirecting efforts that fail to do so. This also brings shareholders and employees into closer personal alignment with the corporate vision and its main strategic objectives.

7. Caring and Crossing: Setting up and supporting an atmosphere of concern and attention (caring) to all internal stakeholders, both as individuals and as parts of the corporate whole. When this atmosphere of caring has spread throughout the organization, it extends (crosses) to external stakeholders (customers, suppliers, and the general community).

This brief outline of the Seven Cs explains what they are and how they interrelate. I will now explore each of them in detail, talk about the indicators that show their presence or absence, and show how a company can gain them or become better at them. Remember the existence of any competency opens the way for (and reinforces) all the others, as in a living organism.

The needs and expectations of the customers and the marketplace change constantly. Healthy, agile, and organic companies sense these changes and continuously transform themselves to respond properly. Because change always causes insecurity, a healthy organization needs solid faith in its ability to respond successfully. This allows the systematic risk-taking that makes success possible. Thus, the first competency that I will analyze is confidence.

Confidence: The Foundation of Everything

Confidence must be present in organizations from the start. It is the founder's confidence in his or her ability to satisfy certain needs in the marketplace that causes him or her to start the organization in the first place. Subsequently, the stakeholders must release, spread, and strengthen this confidence through continuous regeneration and rebirth.

Most founders rely on their belief in their own success and their ability to read the current market to discover who their customers will be, what their needs are, and the products or services that will satisfy those needs. They are confident that the market will provide both demand and continuing capital to allow them to fulfill their purpose, guided by their values and identity.

Confidence comes from the internal stakeholders' belief that they have the ability to design and complete the structure, processes, and products (or services) that will bring the company to its ideal form. For this conviction to exist, it is important that the company and its internal stakeholders have the knowledge, skills, and capital that they need to achieve this result. Top management's chief role always should be to reaffirm this confidence. They must nurture the certainty that the company can achieve the corporate vision and provide the management structure needed to achieve that vision.

To do this, however, the company must have the following in place:

- A program that satisfies the training and development needs of every employee, tailored to each individual role;

- An orientation program that helps a new employee to become productive quickly;

- A direct link between these programs and the core strategic objectives put forward by the corporate vision. That is, all employees have the skills they need to help fulfill these objectives by performing their function in full, specific knowledge of how their work moves the company toward the vision;

- An information network that keeps all internal stakeholders up-to-date on every step the company takes in both its transformation process and the company's day-to-day operations.

As I deconstruct the nature and implementation of the other competencies, I will show how important it is to build a new and lasting organizational sailboat (structure, strategy, and culture) to use to survive the tsunamis of globalization. Organizational Architecture—the carrying out of the transformation—serves as a fundamental resource for developing confidence and maturity within the company. The process uniquely provides sustainable conditions for participative realization of the corporate vision, through targeting and achieving of strategic objectives.

Commitment: Upholding Momentum

A person will found an organization to fulfill a specific customer need. The founder selects the need that this new organization will satisfy and decides how to structure the organization to satisfy those needs. The founder bases these decisions on his or her personal purpose and values system. People will not willingly start an organization whose reason for being or way of doing business violates their personal purpose and values.

Similarly, people choose to work in an organization because of values and purpose. What normally attracts a person to companies is a feeling (conscious or unconscious) that the company's purpose and values align closely with his or her own. They will not willingly join a company whose purpose and values are in conflict with their own.

Commitment is loyalty in thought and behavior. In general, human beings commit only to projects or organizations that fulfill their own purpose and adhere to their own values system. Their loyalty is in proportion to the degree that their work satisfies their personal purpose and agrees with their values system. To have committed employees, the company's purpose and values must closely align with their own. This high level of commitment is obvious in nonprofit organizations where people volunteer for a cause. People work incredibly hard for little compensation, just because they identify so strongly with the organization's purpose!

In the beginning, the founder and the organization are one, and the founder's personal purpose and values *are* the organization's purpose and values. As time passes, the company's early focus starts to expand, and the stakeholders (shareholders, employees, customers, suppliers, and the community) will naturally try to shape the company's purpose and values system. Unless the company recognizes and actively embraces these changes, the stakeholders will lose their commitment, and the company will decline.

To preserve lasting stakeholder commitment, the organization must periodically clarify its purpose statement and values system because of any changes to its stakeholders' purpose and values. As the stakeholders see the organization in closer and closer alignment with their personal purpose and values, they feel increasingly committed to the organization's success.

It is worth noting that for a company to show real commitment, most of the internal stakeholders must already be in the conformist stage of ego development or higher. If most internal stakeholders are at impulsive or opportunistic levels, then they will react to change by freezing and waiting for someone to show them what to do next. Commitment is impossible.

Cocreation: Building the Future through Teamwork

Cocreation is the continual, organization-wide reenactment of the creative process the founder went through when he or she originally set up the company. It is a regular part of daily organizational life. When cocreating, the members of the organization detect the environmental trends that will have an effect on their customers' needs and the company's abilities in the future. They revisit the company's purpose and make certain that it still addresses the needs of their target market, or that the target market still falls within the purpose. They convert the purpose and values into behaviors that will anticipate the clients' needs. Together, they create a corporate vision—a projection of what life in the organization will be like today, tomorrow, and in the next five to ten years. A good vision speaks in the present tense, as if the company had already achieved each of the four vision categories: client interface, transformation, people management, and financial management.

I call this competency cocreation and not creation. I want to differentiate creation, the birth of the company (an act of the founder years ago), from cocreation, a continuous, ongoing activity in which everyone in the organization takes part (see Figure 5).

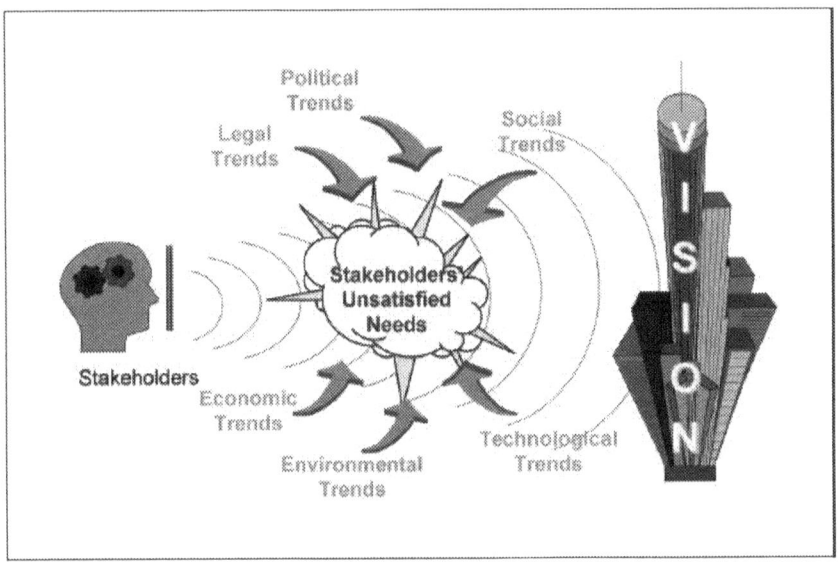

Figure 5: The cocreative process.

As I said earlier, the organization gains or sharpens its ability to scan its environmental horizon for change by practicing cocreation. It learns to recognize the advantages and disadvantages of what it detects and to alter its strategy if necessary based on this information. It uses environmental scans (which I will discuss in detail in Chapter 6) to create a panoramic view of its *opporthreats* (all opportunities contain threats and all threats contain opportunities). Then, using trend analysis, the organization predicts its most probable futures. Based on these predictions, the members of the organization reexamine its purpose and values to make sure that they are still on target and relevant to the new current reality and customer needs. On this firm foundation, they build and continually update a strategic vision of the organization's ideal future. This ensures that it has the agility to meet threats and seize opportunities, thus ensuring its survival in the short and long terms.

It is important to involve all stakeholders (employees, major clients, and shareholders) in cocreating the vision. This is not only because it increases stakeholder confidence and commitment, which is in itself worthwhile; a vision that combines the knowledge and wisdom from all the stakeholders is powerful. To involve everyone in the process, we use large-scale real-time strategy and decision-making techniques, such as Dannemiller Tyson Associates' Whole-Scale methodology. This allows a critical mass of the organization (or a subsystem within the organization) to define the essential parts of the vision while experiencing it directly.

Cocreation is the competency that shifts the model for leadership from the founder to the vision. Instead of following the founder into the future, the stakeholders are fulfilling the vision that they themselves cocreated. Everyone takes part, so every action moves the company toward the vision. Multidisciplinary, cross-cultural task teams comprised of internal stakeholders from different hierarchical levels and functional areas perform specific tasks to help achieve the vision. Company-wide meetings preserve strategic alignment with purpose and values.

Cocreation needs a confident and committed team. All stakeholders must be willing to contribute the best of their knowledge, skills, and ability to build a means of exploring opportunities and detecting threats. Cocreation reinforces the stakeholders' confidence and commitment. Instead of depending on external consultants—all-knowing experts from outside the company—to create their future for them, they create their own success. They start believing in themselves.

I have found that internal teams are much more effective than teams of outsiders, and their successes create confidence and a growing, organization-wide commitment to the values and purpose. After successfully completing its task, each team disbands and its members become the nuclei of new teams involving people from all different areas and levels, diffusing skills and experience throughout the organization. Thus, cocreation becomes a strong part of the company's routine.

Using this approach, a more organic structure safely and gradually replaces the rigid hierarchical system. Stakeholders mature personally, and the company's culture deepens while becoming more agile and better able to deal with the current reality. Because consensus replaces autocracy as the decision-making process, the organization increasingly is able to take advantage of the diversity of stakeholders' points of view and this richness of alternatives. Thus, the company builds stronger muscles, becomes more agile, and loses the rigidity caused by automatic, mechanical responses. These new muscles reinforce the internal stakeholders' confidence and commitment, both to one another as individuals and toward the company. By collectively understanding the present reality and an intended and desired future, the company and all its stakeholders mature.

Connection: The Guarantee of Realism

Connection is the competency of managing the transition from the company's current reality to its future vision. Connection sets up processes, structures, and planning to ensure that the company achieves the vision on schedule. Like cocreation, connection builds the organization's muscles, helping the individuals and the organization to mature. Connection requires the organization to define the steps that it needs to take to achieve the vision, constantly being aware of where it is in relation to the direction it has chosen. Connection requires a clear vision and an honest understanding of the organization's current reality, internal and external. Connection is about thinking in the future while acting in the present. The future pulls us ahead (*future pull*) while the current reality holds us back (I call this *culture suck*, and will talk about it in greater depth in Chapter 5). Like stretching a rubber band, this causes constant internal tension. This tension becomes energy the organization can use to stimulate the activities that move it toward the future.

Connection produces and requires a high degree of emotional maturity. For instance, when we tell children that they must learn to wait for something they want, they can barely control their anxiety. Children act at a less mature stage of development and only believe in what is within reach. They are afraid that their needs will not be met. Being connected implies a firm belief in achieving a future reality within a definite period, while admitting there is still a long way to go. The organization needs maturity to be honest about its current reality and to have the patience and determination to travel the uncharted paths to the future.

Connection is a three-part process:

1. Defining (or redefining) the strategic objectives in terms of purpose, values, and vision;

2. Understanding how the objectives relate to one another; and

3. Understanding the steps the company must take to convert these goals into reality.

It is essential to achieve these objectives through a participative process that creates confidence and focuses the internal stakeholders' commitment.

The vision statement is the key to the strategy. Because we base the vision on the purpose and values, each phrase (element) of an effective vision becomes a key strategic goal. I helped to set up a transition management board

(TMB), which is responsible for fulfilling the strategy. The TMB must consider each vision element and rank it two ways: by its relative importance in the overall picture and by the progress the company has already achieved toward it.

Connection yields a general strategic Transition Map that signals precisely what the company must do to produce their ideal future. The map is based on the vision and is in alignment with the corporate purpose and values. This map identifies the behavior and structures the organization should improve (considering their relative importance and degree of achievement), those it should remove (because they do not align with the corporate vision), and those it should leave alone. The TMB is responsible for this continuing process, starting with the transformation and continuing into the indefinite future.

Connection is always the most difficult competency to carry out—more so than creating confidence, upholding commitment, or cocreating the corporate vision. Connecting creates a noticeable, fundamental shift in the organization's structure. Sudden movements in the ocean floor can create a tsunami; the paradigm shifts that accompany connection can also create huge waves of change within the organization. They can be constructive or destructive, but in any case they will disrupt the status quo.

The sticking point with connection lies in the desire to succumb to inertia when transformation is a strategic necessity. All organisms, including organizations, naturally desire things to stay as they are. On the other hand, all complex systems aspire to realize their full potential. Resistance to change is a normal defense when faced with an unknown and uncertain future. The Spanish have a saying: "Even a bad present that we know is better than a future that we do not!" Accepting an unfavorable—although comfortable—condition instead of taking risks to build a new reality with new possibilities is normal. At times like these, during renewal and reevaluation, conflict surfaces. The future pulls the entire organization forward and upward in pursuit of the new corporate vision, driving change. The old, sucking culture does the exact opposite, struggling against the entire transformation process and obstructing or delaying the necessary changes.

Organizational Architecture ensures that each of the Seven Cs is present in the organization and it helps the organization increase each of them to an optimal level. As we apply Organizational Architecture to establish connection in organizations that have not been practicing this competence, serious resistance begins. It is during connection that the battle between future pull and culture suck is fiercest. While building confidence, commitment, and cocreation, internal stakeholders actively take part in and enjoy the process, even though many believe that it is all just fantasy. In the connection phase, the old culture suddenly realizes that *the transformation is in serious danger of actually succeeding.* This is not just another failed change management project. Organizational Architecture really works!

Individuals at the impulsive, opportunistic, and conformist levels of maturity start resisting when they realize that genuine change has begun—when they notice that an organic values are replacing the traditional hierarchical values. They have watched tolerantly, even helping the process, especially during the high-visibility, successful, and easy activities that build confidence and commitment. Suddenly, when they see true change almost on their doorstep, they set in motion extraordinary efforts to suck the company back into the old ways.

People who have been champions of the transformation suddenly turn against the entire effort. Up to this point, they have seen the process as a vehicle to increase their personal power. Suddenly they realize that achieving the vision will lead to a completely new structure, and (correctly or not) they see their power base eroding. They feel the new order is threatening values and skills that put them where they are today. This leads them to question (often unconsciously) their part in the organizational transformation. Do they have the expertise, skill, and emotional conviction to preserve a similar position and importance in the new structure? What if they do not, and they eventually lose position and power? Thus begins the worst kinds of political and self-protective infighting.

For the transition to succeed, the organization must overcome this resistance immediately and at any cost. It can fatally undermine any possibility of changing the status quo and achieving the ideal future.

The Seven Cs, when present at any level, attenuate the effects of culture suck. Although resistance to change is unavoidable when transforming complex systems, in a healthy transformation it fades with time as the advancement to higher maturity levels leads to positive methods for adapting.

As I said before, the difference between where we are and where we want to be causes tension. Either we convert this tension into directed, motivated, confident, and mature behavior, or it will become fear leading to paralysis.

Communication: The Key to Vitality

Communication keeps the corporate vision aligned with the stakeholders' purpose and values. This reinforces confidence and commitment, allowing for cocreation and connection, eventually fulfilling the organization's objectives.

To keep internal stakeholders committed, everyone should be continuously aware of the progress of the organizational transformation. In the past, this happened periodically: monthly or quarterly. Today, it can and should take place daily or weekly. As we move into the future, it should become a real-time process.

We are living in a world that for almost any decision making is increasingly dependent on "any time, any place" information. The definitions of shopping and travel planning, for instance, are undergoing major transformation. In the past, if we wanted to find a bargain or a hard-to-find product, we might spend hours driving or calling all over town, or perhaps walking around the shopping mall after work in search of it. Today, you can go to a Web site that will search hundreds or thousands of stores, any time of the day or night, and deliver what is conceivably the best deal in the entire world on a particular item.

In addition, it used to be that your travel agent (available only during business hours in one time zone) would find the best deal for your travel plans. Web sites have largely replaced that function, as they search dozens or hundreds of providers to get the best travel deal for you automatically at any hour of the day or night, from anywhere in the world.

People's ability to get the information that they need right now to make the best decisions possible has a strong effect on their expectations, which they naturally bring to the workplace. Thus, agile, competitive companies—those that can detect the tsunami and are preparing for it—are gaining the ability to make information instantly available to their managers and stakeholders. An agile organization, like any live organism, is able to assess threats and opportunities quickly so that it can make the right decisions and take the suitable actions that will help it to compete successfully. Instant access to relevant information makes this possible.

Any organization that wants to remain competitive (or merely survive) in this increasingly real-time and globalized environment must strengthen its own communication competency. Otherwise, it will never fully realize its corporate vision, much less preserve its market share or gain the advantage over competitors.

As the organization begins to connect, people need increasing amounts of information to stay on task and on track. Good information is essential to effective decision making, and the connection phase increases the number of decisions that individuals have to make; they must keep the existing organization alive while simultaneously building a new one. People who have built a new home have had a similar experience.

Not only must the stakeholders make more decisions, but because of the improving communication competency, the results of those decisions (good or bad) become much more visible. Thus, making good decisions (those that move the organization closer to the vision) becomes increasingly important to both the individual and the organization.

The competently communicating organization demands good decisions from the internal stakeholder, who needs and demands from the organization good information to make them. Thus, the need for competent communication becomes circular and self-reinforcing.

Effective communication itself is an opporthreat. In traditional hierarchies, managers make key decisions for employees and often keep them in the dark strategically, so employee information needs are typically low. In an organic structure, individuals are more involved in strategy-driven decision making, and their need to acquire and effectively communicate information is relatively high. Simultaneously, the company starts to become competent in communication, and the available information grows. However, because information is amassing at such a pace, the data themselves are often disorderly and scattered, and thus not as useful to the internal stakeholders as they might be. The challenge now becomes keeping the information organized, useful, and timely. Moreover, because relevant information has been largely unavailable, most people lack the skill to get and use it. They become deluged, disoriented, and despondent. In addition, in most hierarchical organizations, only a few people have ever needed to communicate effectively, and most of these are in management roles. Thus, although a growing number of people need effective communication skills, few have them.

In an organic organization, free and effective (i.e. competent) communication is a fundamental need for individuals at all levels. The first step to achieve this is setting up a vision of effective communications within the organization. The process for this is similar to the visioning process for the entire organization, but focuses only on communication. This is a good opportunity for the organization to gain and apply its new connecting skills to fulfill a vision specifically for communication.

One of the most important vision elements for communication will be the *communications protocol*. The communications protocol is simply the strategy and rules behind each mode of communication used by the organization. Each mode has its own distinct strategy, and its own set of rules. Setting up a good communications protocol is just as important for old-fashioned communication, such as meetings, conversation, telephone, "snail mail," or fax, as it is for the newer, digital communications technologies, such as the Internet, e-mail, workflow automation, and knowledge management. However, because digital media provide richer, more precise, and faster communication than manual methods, the need for protocols for these is greater.

Several benefits of competent communication are:

- Stakeholders can have rapid and easy access to useful information, so that they can respond to opporthreats quickly and competently (i.e., in alignment with the purpose, values, and vision).

- The information flow becomes so relevant that stakeholders become enthusiastic about the act of communication, which in turn brings everyone into greater integration, helping them to mature.

- The organization has clearly defined the rules about the information flow, and everyone understands and accepts them.

- People are free from unorganized, unprioritized, or irrelevant information.

- Individuals and groups know each other's progress, in an easy and confident way that the company supports and encourages.

Communication is the basis for another competence that is essential for consolidating the process, adding coherence among individuals, and increasing their chances of collective success. I will discuss communication in more detail in Chapter 8.

Celebration and Course Correction: The Organizational Rudder

Traditional hierarchies use assessment and correction in a power-based carrot-and-stick combination. They reward "winners" (those who vanquish their counterparts) with increased power and wealth, and punish the "losers" with the opposite. How can they uphold an environment of confidence, commitment, cocreation, connection, and communication if individual successes and mistakes (and power) are more important than achieving the vision?

Organizations need a completely different steering mechanism. Monitoring, assessment, and course correction should focus on progress toward fulfilling the organization's strategy, nothing more, and certainly nothing less. Individual and general successes are those actions that move the organization toward achieving the vision. The organic organization celebrates these. Mistakes are actions that delay or set back the organization in achieving the vision. It learns from these as it corrects them.

Celebration is the natural and indispensable other half of course correction. When the company celebrates positive behavior, people are more able to face their failures and mistakes, admit to them, and learn from them. This mature behavior helps them understand their usefulness and value to the group, which creates confidence, allowing the organization to set increasingly higher individual and team objectives.

The organization coordinates every activity and measures its success through communication; celebration and course correction keep the organization on track and motivated. They mutually strengthen commitment, and they reaffirm the confidence the stakeholders have in one another. They promote continuous cocreation in a reality that is firmly connected to the future.

To celebrate and course correct effectively, the organization needs to:

- Require and define clear objectives and milestones for each activity, continuously targeting the corporate vision.

- Continuously oversee all tasks and missions, based on performance targets previously established as a group.

- Recognize in a public and sincere way every success or victory that moves the organization closer to the vision.

- Encourage an atmosphere of positive feedback, so those responsible can confidently change the course of activities that fail to move the organization toward the vision, without hurt feelings or resentment.

Caring: Making Well-Being Your Ally

The last of the Seven Cs is caring. A wise old saying says, "People take care of what they like." Caring means being concerned for, having regard for and continuously nurturing. I believe that only a caring team of shareholders and employees can nurture, encourage, and preserve a healthy emotional environment within an organization. This becomes a precious asset for the company, whose attitude of respect, caring, and trust eventually extends to the market, significantly benefiting the company's identity (public perception of its purpose and values).

Respect is the basis of caring. It not only includes the respect that the internal stakeholders (employees and shareholders) give the company and its assets, but it also includes the company's respect for *all* its stakeholders (shareholders, employees, customers, and suppliers).

In general, company founders care deeply about every facet of their company, as if it were an extension of them. The founder naturally treats employees as part of the family. Customers are very important people, and the company is always open to suggestions for improvement. Founders zealously care for assets; they evolve relations with suppliers in an atmosphere of continuous mutual respect, trust, and open dialog. Like a carefully nurtured flower, the company blooms under this constant care, leading to an atmosphere of confidence and commitment that extends beyond the company's walls, linking and delighting customers, suppliers, and other partners.

As a company grows, the number of people who become involved increases, and the growing variety of individual values, purposes, and visions for the future gradually replace those of the founder. Caring attitudes become impersonal performance indicators. The respect and concern for stakeholders dampens, whether internal (shareholders and employees) or external (customers, suppliers, and the community).

It is fundamentally important to create conditions that allow the recovery and improvement of this caring attitude throughout the company and its stakeholders. Repeatedly working through the Seven Cs builds caring as the result. Alternatively, without caring, the other Seven Cs are unsustainable in the long term.

The Optimal Organization

With these seven essential competencies in place, the company continually transforms itself from the inside out into a more agile, mature, and organic organization, using its own resources and skills. It constantly strives to carry out a corporate vision, cocreated by its dedicated, committed, mature, and productive stakeholders. It promotes an atmosphere of equality, respect, and caring, in a culture that motivates, produces well-being, and adds value to the organization, the internal stakeholders, and the community.

The Organizational Architecture process of transformation respects the organization's own character and uniqueness to avoid disrupting the existing structure while building the new one. Thus, each organization uniquely sets up each of the Seven Cs. There is no right or wrong implementation; success is simply increased competence in each of the seven areas.

There is no specific moment in which the corporate vision becomes finished. Just as the stakeholders never stop maturing, neither does the organization ever become fully competent in all seven competencies. It can only increase its level of each competency every time it passes through the Seven Cs. As the organization revisits its purpose and values; rescans the environment; redefines its vision; becomes more effective at communicating; celebrates new successes; course-corrects new, less successful efforts; and lavishes more caring on itself and its stakeholders, these competencies become stronger. The organization moves closer to its ideal, optimal condition.

Optimal organizations have the following characteristics:

- The organization bases its purpose on its values system and the specific needs of its customers, supporting successful interaction among internal and external stakeholders (shareholders, employees, customers, suppliers, and the community).

- The corporate vision statement is a clear, comprehensive picture of what life will be like in the company on a certain day in the future.

- The corporate vision is the ideal future expression of the company's purpose and values, based on a sharp awareness of trends in the business environment and the marketplace.

- Everyone in the organization knows the specific steps that it will need to take to achieve the vision and is motivated to do so because of his or her strong personal alignment with it.

- The corporation is led by its vision statement, which it uses as a guiding light to stay on course into the future.

- Shareholders and employees take pride in being creators of the future rather than inheritors of the past.

- People are confident the organization can deal with any challenge it might face.

- Shareholders and employees are skilled at converting the current reality into the goals and tasks that move the company toward the corporate vision.

- Employees receive information through training programs that are relevant to the skills they need to achieve their part of the corporate vision; new employees quickly gain the knowledge and skills that they need to become productive.

- The organization has a useful and precise communications system that enables it to coordinate and spread information quickly and effectively, keeping everyone apprised of how individual and collective tasks are progressing in real time.

- Shareholders and employees understand that effective communication in support of the business processes is essential for achieving the corporate vision.

- Communication is universally effective within the organization, and people enjoy communicating; they know that communication technology is more than electronics—it is a combination of scientific principles and knowledge applied to any human interaction.

- There are objective performance indicators to assess each specific goal and milestone leading toward the corporate vision.

- A system based on the corporate identity, values, purpose, and vision continuously fed by customer feedback identifies, highlights, and rewards exceptional performance. It also points to course corrections, and supplies inputs for periodic reviews of the corporate purpose and vision.

- The organization encourages shareholders and employees to give feedback in an open and positive manner, creating an atmosphere that celebrates successes, invites risk taking, and welcomes course correction as a part of the process.

- The organization supports an atmosphere of caring for customers, suppliers, colleagues, products, tools, and facilities that creates internal contentment.

- The organization extends trust, caring, and mutual respect to everyone with whom it interacts. This reinforces an attitude of esteem for others and for self (by reaffirming its peak condition as creator), resulting in a positive image in the business environment (attracting talents, promoting alliances, and creating opportunities).

There is another benefit to striving for the ideal state. Organizations have much power and influence on the communities in which they exist. Therefore, I believe that organizations can help to change the hierarchical values system that has prevailed in our culture until the present day and has resulted in so much strife and unrest. This will help people to become more mature and decrease the potential for tsunamis of resentment that erupt from conditions of immaturity and inequality.

Chapter 5

Renewal Through Organizational Architecture

In the last chapter, I explained the Seven Cs and how they can be used to build an optimal organization. In this chapter, I will talk about the logical framework behind Organizational Architecture and how my colleagues and I developed it.

Renewing Complex Organizations

As I said in Chapter 3, the wave of change is already washing away organizations that cannot or will not learn how to sail through it. Traditional companies, with their hierarchical processes and structures, cannot survive the tsunami. It is futile to improve hierarchy because the underlying principles are obsolete. *There is no way to make a hierarchy strong and agile enough to survive a tidal wave.* The only way that any organization can guarantee its survival is to build a new, organic organizational structure, a sailboat, designed "from the keel up" to sail tsunamis.

Now, this statement goes against common wisdom. Everyone knows, for instance, that you cannot change an entire organization. This is especially the case for people who have been through a process-improvement-style change program. They watched specialists reengineer the processes, and then over time they watched the company return to its old ways. These people, these veterans, *know* that lasting change is impossible. Nevertheless, they are wrong! I have proven repeatedly that Organizational Architecture will successfully change an organization, giving it an organic, tsunami-sailing structure in the short-term and the ability to continually redefine and renew itself in the long-term. Traditional methods for transforming management structures undertake to improve the present state, whereas Organizational Architecture builds the future.

These are bold claims. To justify them, I will give a short history of the development of Organizational Architecture.

Understanding How Organizational Architecture Evolved

As I said earlier in the book, it all started in Curaçao. After the uprising, the business and social leaders of the island started a think tank called *Fundashon Renovashon* (of which I was a part) to study the causes behind the riots and find a means to prevent them from happening again. At the *Fundashon*, we asked the following questions of thousands of Antilleans, and the vast majority answered as shown:

Q. What happened?

A. People rebelled and protested with violence.

Q. Why did they do this?

A. Because the company treated them as if they were incompetent.

Q. Why did the company treat them this way?

A. The company said that they were not as productive as were their counterparts in more developed countries.

Q. What was the basis of this assertion?

A. The company told them they lacked motivation.

Based on these results, we decided to study motivation and see how we could help the Antilleans become more motivated at work. As I said in Chapter 3, my colleagues and I turned to the work of Dr. David McClelland of Harvard University and *achievement motivation*. In his research, he had shown that companies made up of achievement-motivated people grow faster and were more profitable than those whose members lack achievement motivation. He also related superior national economic growth to the presence of a large percentage of achievement-motivated individuals in the country. We felt that if we could help the people of Curaçao to become more achievement-motivated, the individuals, the companies, and indeed the entire nation would benefit.

During the 1960s, McClelland had successfully instilled the achievement motive in people in India and in certain inner-city areas in the United States. We asked him and his team to help us train Curaçao's entire population to be achievement-motivated. Working with McClelland's group, we created a personal-development program based on his earlier studies and began training a cross-section of the Antillean population. Everyone—sponsors, trainers, and participants—worked hard and invested heavily in the program.

After we had put several hundred people through the program, we took an interim look at the results. We had expected a general uplifting of the awareness among the participants in the training. The results differed drastically from our expectations. We found that people reacted to the training in three different ways.

One group became achievement-motivated, as McClelland had predicted. This group, because of the new skills that they had gained, rapidly gained stature in their communities. Understandably, they were pleased with the results of the training, and we were satisfied with the changes that we had wrought in their lives. These people had positive effects on their various communities, and this was encouraging to us.

Our efforts with the other two groups did not deliver such positive returns, however. The second group interpreted the achievement techniques as a means to increase their personal power. They became adept at manipulation and other negative behavior, and had a negative effect on their communities. This more or less neutralized the positive influence of the first group. The third group was apparently unaffected by the training. For some reason, this group received no benefit from what we were trying to do, and the training made no difference in their personal or community life. This was the most unfortunate result, because this group was by far the largest of the three, well over half of the total group.

Based on these observations, we saw that this effort to make the island's population achievement-motivated was doomed to failure. If we continued to provide our training to the rest of the population, we would produce a small group of achievers that would raise the society's overall motivation level. We would simultaneously create a group of people skilled in personal power motivation that would drag it back down. Furthermore, the major result of our efforts would be to waste the time of a large number of people.

Another interesting outcome—and a very important one—was the later experience of the first group (who had become more achievement-motivated) when they returned to their jobs. We hoped that this group would justify some of the time and money that we had spent by improving the productivity of their organizations as McClelland's research had promised. Unfortunately, this did not happen. After they returned to work, not only did their company *not* experience any improvement in productivity, many from this group quit their jobs to go into business for themselves (some very successfully). The ones that stayed behind became miserable and unproductive. We asked some of them what had gone wrong. They said that after they returned to their old jobs, their managers expected them to behave in their old ways. The organization's top management had requested achievement-motivated workers, but when it got them, the existing organizational structure would not allow achievement-motivated behavior. This left the workers feeling betrayed, purposeless, and angry. It eventually forced many of them to leave the company. Our training program was therefore unsuccessful in achieving the strategy of making employees more productive.

These results were disappointing. Several of us, including Harry Lasker, founded a new organization, *Fundashon Humanas*, to take our research in a new direction. Our purpose was still to find a reliable method for building an achievement-motivated society, but our first order of business was to understand what had gone wrong with our previous efforts.

Although we still believed in McClelland's achievement motivation theory, we used two theories (mentioned earlier in the book) to find out why we had not achieved the results we expected. They were Jane Loevinger's "Ego Stages," which I presented in detail in Chapter 3, and Julian B. Rotter's "Locus of Control," specifically the creature and creator feelings mentioned in Chapter 1. From the authors' writings and our own experiences, we suspected there were linkages and likenesses among all three. This would help to explain why our achievement motivation training failed.

We measured thousands of people in Curaçao, Caracas, London, New York, and elsewhere using Loevinger's, Rotter's, and McClelland's instruments and found a strong correlation among all three theories. We proved that individuals with low ego development (immaturity) according to Loevinger's scale (the impulsive, opportunistic, and conformist stages) also lacked achievement motivation in McClelland's terminology. Furthermore, they felt externally controlled, according to Rotter's Social Learning Theory. They saw themselves as pawns in the chess game of life, and creatures of fate, believing that they were victims of chance, bad luck, destiny, or any force outside their control. On the other hand, those that had reached the higher stages of self-awareness and maturity (conscientious, autonomous, and integrated according to Loevinger) were achievement-motivated. They also perceived themselves as determiners of their own destiny, creators of their desired future, in Rotter's terms.

Figure 6 shows that the creature and creator lines intersect at a point between Loevinger's conformist and conscientious ego stages, a point that she calls the *self-aware transitional stage*. This is a point of significant personal change. It is where the individual becomes truly self-aware. It is a point of opportunity and threat to the individual. Creature energy and creator energy are in balance. A slight movement toward conscientious would lead to a quantum step in personal growth. However, the individual has a significant investment in the hierarchical values system and thinks hierarchically. In most situations, he or she will try to keep things as they are. On the other hand, an individual at this stage can easily become more achievement-motivated through training such as we gave in Curaçao.

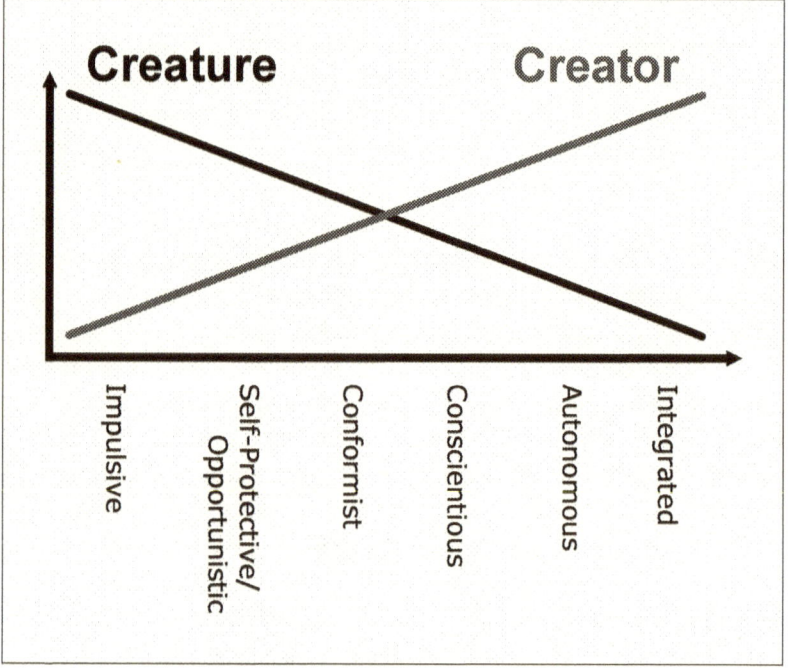

Figure 6: Creature versus creator behavior as
a function of ego development stage.

This explained why our achievement-motivation training worked well on some, produced the opposite effect on a second group, and had no effect on the rest. The ones who benefited from the training were people who were already at the self-aware stage. The opportunists saw the new skills as a way to take advantage of the large number of conformists, and the conformists received no benefit at all.

Although we had explained how maturity affected achievement motivation, we still did not know why some adults were at one ego stage, while others were at a lower or higher ego stage. For instance, why would one person behave at the opportunistic level, while another of the same age act at the con-scientious level? Obviously, maturity was not dependent on chronology. Once again, Julian Rotter's work—this time, his Social Learning Theory (1954)—helped us to understand. He introduced the idea that a person becomes stuck at a certain developmental level. Rotter said that during life you build up certain beliefs that control your behavior, and the more experience reinforces these beliefs, the harder it is for you to change or grow. Fritz Perls's Gestalt Therapy (1969) supported this. Gestalt Therapy says that people with less developed egos swallow what others (such as parents, teachers, authorities, and society) spew at them. They endlessly repeat the decisions that external sources of authority make.

So how could we help those at lower ego stages become more mature? Obviously, achievement-motivation training would not work on immature egos. Rotter tells us that if you want to change a person's behavior, you change the person's environment. Certain structuralists, such as Ichak Adizes, had been using a similar theory that said, "Improved structures promote improved behavior" (Adizes, 1988). I decided to work with Adizes and test this theory.

Basic Roles for Success

According to Adizes, every organization needs to fulfill four basic roles to be successful:

P (Producer), by which the organization carries out its purpose in develop-ing the product or service that best satisfies the needs of its current customers, thus assuring short-term capacity.

A (Administrator), through which the organization guarantees that short-term capacity is transformed into short-term efficiency as it certifies that the "right things" are always produced in the best way possible, by organizing, classifying, watching, and controlling processes.

E (Entrepreneur), though which the organization anticipates trends and identifies the future needs of its customers, the future characteristics of its market, and how the organization itself will look to bring this about. This role promotes the generation of new ideas, processes, and products, aimed at assuring long-term capacity.

I (Integrator), through which the organization aligns and coordinates internal areas and roles, creating a team spirit by transforming individual objectives into common objectives. The integrator role stimulates the group to act as a whole, without depending only on a single area or role, thus assuring its long-term efficiency.

Most companies have strong P and A functions, especially those with large-scale production and complex internal processes. These companies limit the E role to research and development and the I role to the human resource department.

On several projects in North and South America, we made structural improvements to several large, multinational organizations. We strengthened the E and I processes and streamlined the P and A functions, with excellent results. Not only was it possible to change the organizational structure, but also with proper balancing of the PAEI functions, the change could result in immediate, significant increases in productivity.

However, in the long-term, we saw productivity drop again. After much observation and analysis, we realized that even though we had put in place a more efficient structure, most of the people in the company continued to be creatures. They felt externally controlled and behaved according to a hierarchical values system. They were unable or unwilling to use the improved structure properly over the long-term. The existing culture eventually pulled them back into their old behaviors, despite the changes that we had made.

We had discovered a corollary to the structuralist theory that said, "Improved structures promote improved behavior." Our corollary said, "Improved structures promote improved *creature* behavior." What this means is that if you improve (mature) the structure around the people who work in it without also helping them to mature (become *creators*), they will continue to be *creatures*. They will keep acting at low levels of productivity and will continue to be resentful. They will resist change and will eventually revert to less mature structures.

Culture Suck

In most organizations worldwide, the opportunistic and conformist thinking of their members reinforces the hierarchical values and heavily influences their structure, behavior, and culture. By nature, the hierarchical thinking of individuals at the conformist level will try to preserve a status quo. Individuals base their identity on the position they have achieved in the organization or in society and value the struggle that they endured to get there. If anyone tries to make major changes to the organization, this threatens their identity, and so they resist. As I mentioned in Chapter 3, the people at these lower ego stages by nature will fight any effort to bring new ideas into the organization. In particular, they will zealously defend against changes to the structure that supports their personal power and identity.

I call this *culture suck*. Most organizations suffer from it. Any effort to change the existing hierarchical structure around the conformist inhabitants would be certain to fail. The people who have a conformist personality are unable to see the outcome clearly, and the possibility of losing their position in the structure frightens them. At these stages, people try to avoid the tensions of the creative process. It is not easy for conformists to endure the discomfort of change, because their perspective is short-term. They lack the interdependence needed for proper integration of strategy and action. Thus, the culture sucks the individual back into the old structure, canceling change.

A Clean Piece of Paper

How could we overcome culture suck? Structurally, we needed gradual improvement of the E and I roles within the company by consciously stimulating the growth and maturity of managers and employees so they could adequately perform them. Eventually the company would integrate these roles with the P and A roles; that is, the organization's actions would become consistent with its strategy. Such a result, however, depended on all internal stakeholders becoming more mature and learning how to work in a caring, agile, and integrated way.

We saw that building a new structure alongside the old one, in a separate space, protected it from the old culture both physically and ideologically. Thus, the change could occur. If the new structure had an organic values system that would allow for growth, development, and agility, then it could allow more mature individuals in it. If the process itself would help the people within the organization to mature, then it would be simply a matter of moving from the old structure to the new one. In this way, the organization could grow and mature in a lasting way. As the stakeholders pick up new tools and skills, their resistance becomes productive energy, a precious resource for achieving the strategic objectives the company has set for itself.

The resulting transition process gives the company greater entrepreneurial and integrative competence. This is only possible in an atmosphere that involves all internal stakeholders in creating the steps needed to achieve an organic management model. When done well, the prevailing rigid hierarchical values disappear and a new, more organic organization emerges.

Gradual Transformation

Remember that it takes energy to keep character armor—whether personal or organizational—in place. The organization must carefully soften and dissolve this resistance if the transformation process is to succeed. The transformation cannot be abrupt or imposed from the outside. Rather, it must happen gently and gradually, from the inside out. This happens naturally, as the organization gradually moves to higher stages of maturity through better management and maturing of its internal stakeholders.

The process of building the new organization will simultaneously develop the Seven Cs. The stakeholders learn to think and act strategically while building a team spirit and a continuous learning organization (in Adizes' terms it works on building both E and I in the organization). Eventually it integrates these with the production and administrative functions that the company has standardized throughout its years of existence. More than that, the processes it uses will lead to building the muscles the individuals and organization need to grow and mature in an autonomous and integrated way.

Renewal starts with a detailed diagnosis of the company's internal situation. The diagnosis highlights and explains the organization's specific characteristics, including its strengths and weaknesses. In addition, by scanning the business environment, the organization learns more about the external factors that affect its current reality and its future. In practice, the starting point for renewal is the blank sheet of paper. It records the corporate vision shared by internal stakeholders, identifying what they would like the company to become by a specific point in the future, making the dream come true.

This is why Organizational Architecture focuses on building a desired future rather than merely trying to perfect the past. As in a home renovation project, the architect and his or her client exhaustively discuss what the ideal house should be like before putting pencil to paper. Then they decide which parts of the old structure do not work and how the new design will replace them. They identify the parts of the old house that worked well and include them in the new design. Although the owner may want to build the new house around present furniture, home appliances, and decorative objects, the old house must in no way limit the project's potential.

Why We Chose Teams

In the 1970s, my colleagues and I were exploring different ways to stimulate growth and maturity simultaneously in the individuals and the organization. We knew that a more mature organizational structure would be necessary for mature behavior, but we needed a way to build one. "Teams" were currently in vogue in the organizational development field. In a society that is in the conformist stage, as in the 1970s and early 1980s, a team is a place where people can satisfy their acceptance needs. It is not surprising that teams were so popular.

We naturally thought about using teams as the medium for change in our process. However, we knew that if teams did not have the right composition and structure, they would reinforce conformist behavior. For our purposes, therefore, we needed teams that would build self-aware and conscientious behavior.

We knew from McClelland, Loevinger, Rotter, and Adizes that mature, achievement-motivated people thought and acted strategically. Because structure influences behavior, we gave each team a mission that related directly to achieving the corporate strategy. This ensured that the members of the team acted strategically; they would be "building the cathedral," achieving the vision. The mature structure would help the members of the team learn to think and behave strategically. They would also achieve success through this mature behavior, giving them positive reinforcement. At the same time, working on the team increased the individuals' value to the organization by giving them skills, knowledge, and information, thus increasing the team members' feelings of job security.

Over the course of the transition program, a person will work on several teams. As each team achieves success in their mission, they also experience acceptance by their peers. This dispels the idea that acceptance only happens in one group, team, or setting, and satisfies their need for acceptance. Working on a purposeful task in a secure way helps to satisfy their security need. This combination helps individuals satisfy their basic needs and frees them to grow to the self-aware stage and beyond, according to Maslow's theory.

The organization must carry out the transformation through the teamwork of its own stakeholders, supported by specific coaching from those managing the transition. Often purpose, values, and identity are not clear at the start of the process. The old, persistent hierarchical values system and the habits that are characteristic of the less mature ego stages often forbid anyone but top management to think about such "important" issues. In practice, I believe that management should go through the process of defining the company's identity and values, define its purpose, and build a preliminary corporate vision. This includes scanning the environment, analyzing opportunities and threats, negotiating priorities and needs, and identifying shortages and bottlenecks in internal and external business processes. Once management defines the initial strategy, they should involve all stakeholders, or at the least a large, representative cross-section of them, to reaffirm and revise it. After all, no one knows the company as well as do its own stakeholders.

Besides, there is only one way that the company can get real commitment from the stakeholders toward the proposed organizational transformation. Those whom the process will affect directly must feel that they are in control of the process itself (when they can grasp and wield their own power). This is when they stop being creatures of fate and begin to feel they are active creators of change. Because the process includes the layers within the organization that a hierarchical management system would ignore, tensions and unrest decrease. Gradually, everyone—shareholders, employees, suppliers, and the community—learn a more participative way of living, producing, and doing business together.

Organizational Architecture is unlike traditional change management models, where external transformation experts develop an all-inclusive, efficient set of processes for the company to adopt. They base their decisions on their own view of the company and their own benchmarks, and they use proprietary methods for diagnosis, planning, implementation, and control. Organizational Architecture, on the other hand, helps the organization to develop its own new procedures from the collective knowledge of the company's stakeholders. Coaches and other experts may help, but the decisions come from the internal stakeholders.

It is essential that stakeholders have a distinct opportunity to work together in multidisciplinary teams, using the resources and information that are already available within the organization. This is the only way to bring about the collective self-maturing that the organization needs to replace the hierarchy with an organic values system! My colleagues and I have facilitated this process in companies all over the world, and the result has been a heightened shareholder and employee commitment, moving the organization toward the desired future. This self-analysis, self-design, and self-implementation is what allows the organization's maturity to develop, reinforcing its muscles, and preparing it to seize the opportunities and face any threats that a tsunami may bring.

Thus, the organizational transformation promotes the company's maturity. It establishes culture changes, and it becomes a learning and adaptive organization, able to sense opporthreats and quickly transform itself to any extent necessary to use them to its own advantage. The company matures healthily and confidently, with the heightened skills that it needs to realize its full potential. The organizational transformation is a structuring and developing process that touches four basic areas—strategy, structure, culture, and communication—to build an organization of people who are continually creating their own desired future.

Only organizations (and communities) that act at the conscientious, autonomous, and integrated stages can achieve the organic structure that a tsunami-sailing organization needs. Only the higher ego stages show the increased levels of motivation, agility, self-appraisal, interdependence, and self-realization that are reflected in a notably more natural, altruistic, and honest attitude.

The work of George Land on organizational life cycles (1986) supported our conclusion. He even showed that civilization as a whole (not only companies in Curaçao) were at a breakpoint where they were either going to re-create or die (Land, 1992).

Life Cycles and Breakpoints

Organizational life cycles can give us a good picture of how individuals and organizations mature, and breakpoints explain why we use Organizational Architecture to build a new structure alongside the old one. Land goes on to explain why breakpoints are important.

George Land's discoveries, influenced by quantum mechanics and chaos theory, suggest that all living organisms are complex systems. In order to develop, all complex systems go through three phases: forming, norming, and fulfilling. You can see a diagram of these phases in Figure 7.

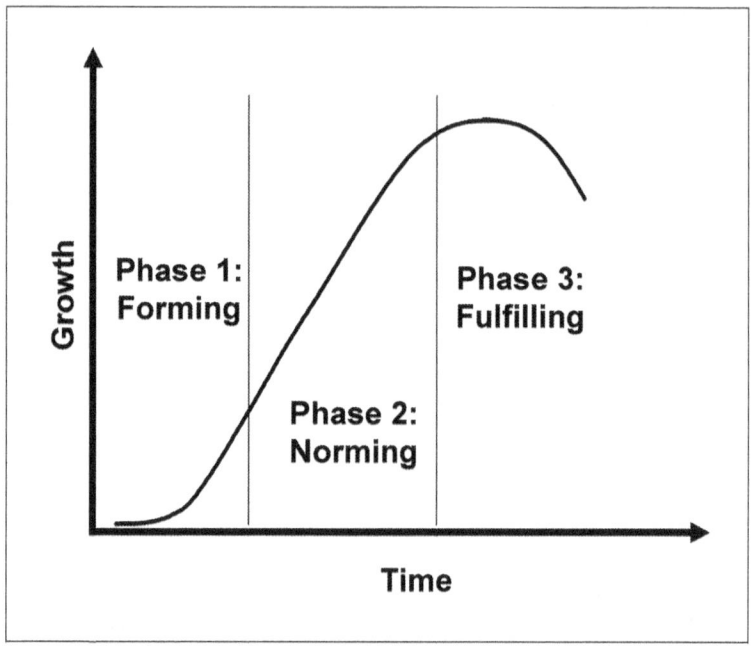

Figure 7: Land's phases of organizational development.

The formation phase corresponds to the organization's birth. It is a chaotic period, when the organization identifies its scope of activity and sets up its fundamental interactions with its environment. Because it has discovered how to serve its customers successfully based on its own values system (thus asserting its identity and purpose), the company continuously tries to confirm that it is doing its best. This explains why interaction with customers and suppliers is so significant in this phase, just as the interaction between shareholders and employees is important.

Few companies, however, survive this forming phase, because everything is new and only just taking shape. Those that do survive normally experience a strong feeling of being special and nothing seems beyond their reach. Everything that one such company does supports its purpose and reaffirms its values, thus continuously satisfying its customers.

However, the company soon realizes that to continue serving its customers well—and thus survive—it must standardize and organize its processes. This will expand its scope and give it the ability to reproduce its success systematically. This is when Phase 2 starts.

In Phase 2, the company sets up standards and procedures that allow it to repeat its profitable activities, ensuring continued success and continued existence. It creates a clearly defined—yet flexible—structure to consolidate its activities. Thus, the organization moves into what Adizes terms "prime."

In this part of Phase 2, the company refines structures and processes. It sees the need for internal integration and interdependence with its stakeholders (employees, shareholders, customers, and suppliers), whether to identify and seize opportunities or to form alliances against threats. Its scope of action gradually expands and its vulnerability increases.

Now the company starts to move into the end of Phase 2, where it takes advantage of all the gains and improvements that it made earlier in Phase 2. Because the structures and processes that it has been refining have proven successful, it starts to treat them as infallible, carved in stone, and the company's only guarantee of survival. The organization starts to take its success for granted. It is almost collapsing under the weight of the standards and rules it set up in the previous phase. It is becoming sluggish. It cannot integrate itself either internally or externally at the levels needed for continued growth, and this threatens its survival.

This exact moment of going from Phase 2 to Phase 3 is delicate and important, and the organization must decide what it needs to do to survive. Many organizations choose to refine and tighten existing processes. If they do this well, they get a temporary jump in productivity—only to see sluggishness and unresponsiveness reappear over time. The hierarchical values system that has governed the organization since its early phases reasserts itself, suffocating creativity and preventing change.

If you look again at the Figure 7, you will notice that as the organization progresses through Phase 3, the fulfilling phase, it goes into decline. Eventually it will die. This is because, Land says, to stay alive, every living organism must continuously advance to increasingly higher levels of complexity, integration, and interdependence. If the organization stops growing, its flexibility and vital energy will drain away, and its customers will go elsewhere. It will gradually wither until it dies, or until a more effective organization gobbles up the remains.

To effect a true change, the organization must experience rebirth, getting rid of the processes that are holding it back and adopting unprecedented corporate behaviors. It must challenge its previous beliefs and past methods. If the organization manages to free itself from the load of the past, it can achieve a successful transition through fundamental re-creation (the new Phase 3 shown in Figure

8). This can result in a new, highly advanced organism that can deal with the present while preparing to face the future with greater agility.

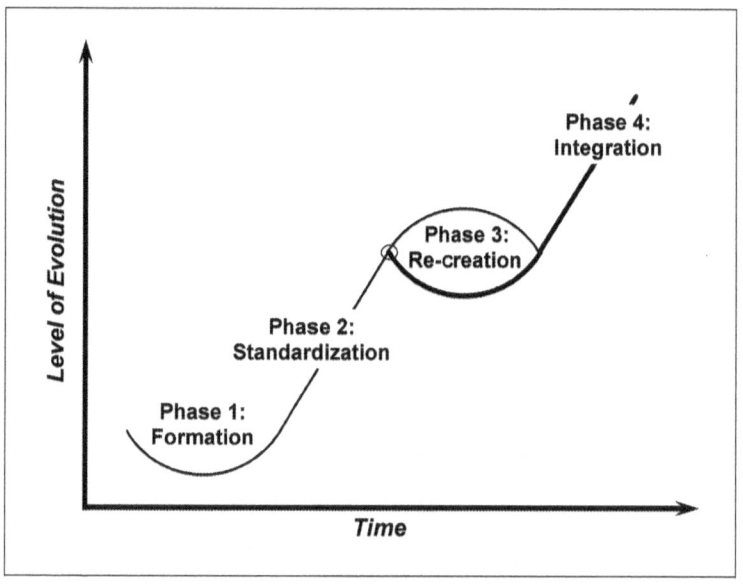

Figure 8: Rebirth of an organization.

The new organization, because it is new, must reexperience the forming and norming phases, but at a higher overall degree of integration. Thus, from the start, it has increased survivability, responsiveness, flexibility, and internal integration between what it is (identity) and what it does. Nevertheless, at some future time, it will once again need to renew itself. Thus, it continuously moves in a cycle of Forming → Norming → Re-Creation.

Most organizations have continued standardizing and managing without realizing that they are at an important point in their history. However, if they do not create a new organization in parallel with the old one, they will die. We call this "change or die" point a *breakpoint*.

We believe we are at an important breakpoint, pressured by information technology on one hand and by the prevailing rigid hierarchical values system on the other. Our organizations are at a decision point. They must either re-create themselves or become extinct. Only those that adapt to a new set of business ideas and approaches will flourish.

Chapter 6

Beginning the Renewal Process

In Chapter 5, I discussed the theoretical framework of Organizational Architecture, and how my colleagues and I discovered it. Chapter 5 showed in greater depth the need for an organically structured organization. In this chapter, I will show how an organization begins the process of re-creation or rebirth.

Any Organization Can Re-create Itself

You may be thinking that an organizational transformation such as the one we propose here would be difficult to carry out. Perhaps you feel that your company's uniqueness would make the process hopelessly complicated. You may even believe, as many people do, that human beings are born to live and work in power hierarchies. Thus, it would be impossible to take a complex organization that has always been a power hierarchy and reinvent it into a nonhierarchical or organic system.

This is not the case. In *every* intervention that we have performed, the success or failure of the organizational transformation hinged on one factor only: the company's willingness to persevere. Technical or procedural issues have little effect on the outcome if top management remains committed to success. Whenever a hierarchical organization makes a sincere commitment to transform itself into an organic one, the transformation succeeds.

I will now show how reinvention can apply to any organization. I will also show that the company must protect the new structure from contamination by the company's old culture.

Guarding against Resistance

Just as a baby needs protection against environmental influences that are harmful to its safe growth, organizational transformation projects need protection from the organization's existing culture. Otherwise, the old culture will undermine the transformation, regardless of how strongly top management supports it. It will become, in the eyes of the stakeholders, yet another failed consultancy project.

My colleagues and I have shown that most internal stakeholders (and thus the organizations that they comprise) work at lower stages of ego development: opportunistic and conformist on the Loevinger scale. People and organizations at the lower ego stages in general think power-hierarchically. They expect management to be nonparticipative and have excessive attachment to preestablished roles. However, in the global economy, this way of thinking is dwindling because it obstructs creativity and interdependence, reducing the flexibility that organizations need for successful business and partnerships.

Any organization's culture will naturally try to neutralize unfamiliar forces that threaten to destabilize the status quo. This is especially true for elitist hierarchies. The old culture exerts pressure on the new to fall back into the old ways, just as mud sucks the foot back into the old footprint. As I said in the previous chapter, culture suck becomes a serious threat to organizational transformation processes. It often causes conflict between the company's opportunistic-conformist culture and the effort to achieve organic maturity. An organization in transformation must therefore carefully protect the new structure, helping the essential competencies to develop (and shaping the company's new sailboat).

The endgame of this transformation effort is not so much remodeling the company's processes as it is helping the stakeholders to become more mature personally. Mature individuals want and need a more mature organization and will work to create and preserve one. Of course, a more mature organizational structure improves the organization's ability to compete, survive, and thrive.

As mentioned in Chapter 3, individuals can become more mature only after satisfying the needs of previous, less mature stages. As individuals mature, their needs change from physical safety and social acceptance to self-appraisal, interdependence, and self-realization. This boosts the collective ability to put in place, strengthen, and extend new ways for working together, production, and doing business in general. This launches the organization into a continuous learning process. Because companies have significant impact on societies, this more creative, respectful, productive, and sustainable culture will eventually spread out on a planetary scale.

Re-creation, an Act of Courage

The first (and most significant) step toward effective organizational change is for the top management of the organization—president, officers, and directors—to decide, firmly and unwaveringly, to make the transformation succeed. They must provide unwavering leadership in the transformation from hierarchical structure into an organic one. They must be prepared to overcome short-term challenges and setbacks to achieve the strategic objective.

The method that they will use is also important, because all the stakeholders must be involved in creating new ways of working together. The company's leaders must be fearless, considering that the transformation will affect the organization at its deepest and most basic levels. It will drive out the hierarchical system of values that has so far prevailed, shattering the company's cultural and personal belief structures!

Furthermore, implanting the necessary competencies in the organization will constantly challenge its members to become ever more mature. As the members mature, they will need and create more mature organizational structures and ever more competency in each of the seven key areas. This is how the transformation process gains steam, and why it is so important to stay on course. It would be a disaster to complete the transformation only partway, maturing the stakeholders in new and exciting ways, and then suddenly forcing them back into the older, immature, hierarchical system.

Because the transformation threatens established power structures, it can be frightening to managers who have used or overcome the hierarchy to achieve their positions of status. This is another part of culture suck. It is also scary for them to think about fundamentally changing an accepted organizational structure and culture. Sometimes, large corporations limit the transformation to a single division before extending it to the entire organization. This successful pilot program not only gives top management confidence, but it also helps convince the other stakeholders that the process will work for the entire organization. Please note that in this circumstance it is essential for the agents of change in that specific division to have the power and authority to complete the necessary tasks successfully.

The transformation team must ensure that internal stakeholders are aware that the organization's culture will undergo a deep and lasting transformation.

It will involve drastic change in communication, management, and consciousness within the company and will entail months of hard work. Thus, significant commitment at the company's highest levels is essential to avoid a shipwreck in the waves of resistance that will surely emerge.

Whatever the company, effective implementation of lasting healthy growth is impossible without achieving four fundamental goals:

1. To promote significant improvement of the company's production, management, and commercial processes;

2. To transform the company from a mechanism into an organism that continually learns and continuously re-creates itself by reinventing its processes and helping its internal stakeholders to mature;

3. To set up a committed and caring team spirit among internal stakeholders, thus allowing, promoting, and supporting agility and continuous improvement;

4. To help internal stakeholders advance from being *creatures* of fate to being *creators* of their own futures, strengthening their commitment toward the company.

Several interrelated tasks make these goals part of the organization's reality. Table 4 shows an example, although the transformation often does not need all the phases. We must adapt the model to the specific characteristics of each organization and its particular setting. Depending on the organization's maturity level, specific characteristics, and internal structure during the transformation, certain tasks might reveal themselves as unnecessary, whereas others may call for more effort than initially expected.

Table 4: An Example of Phases of Transformation Using Organizational Architecture

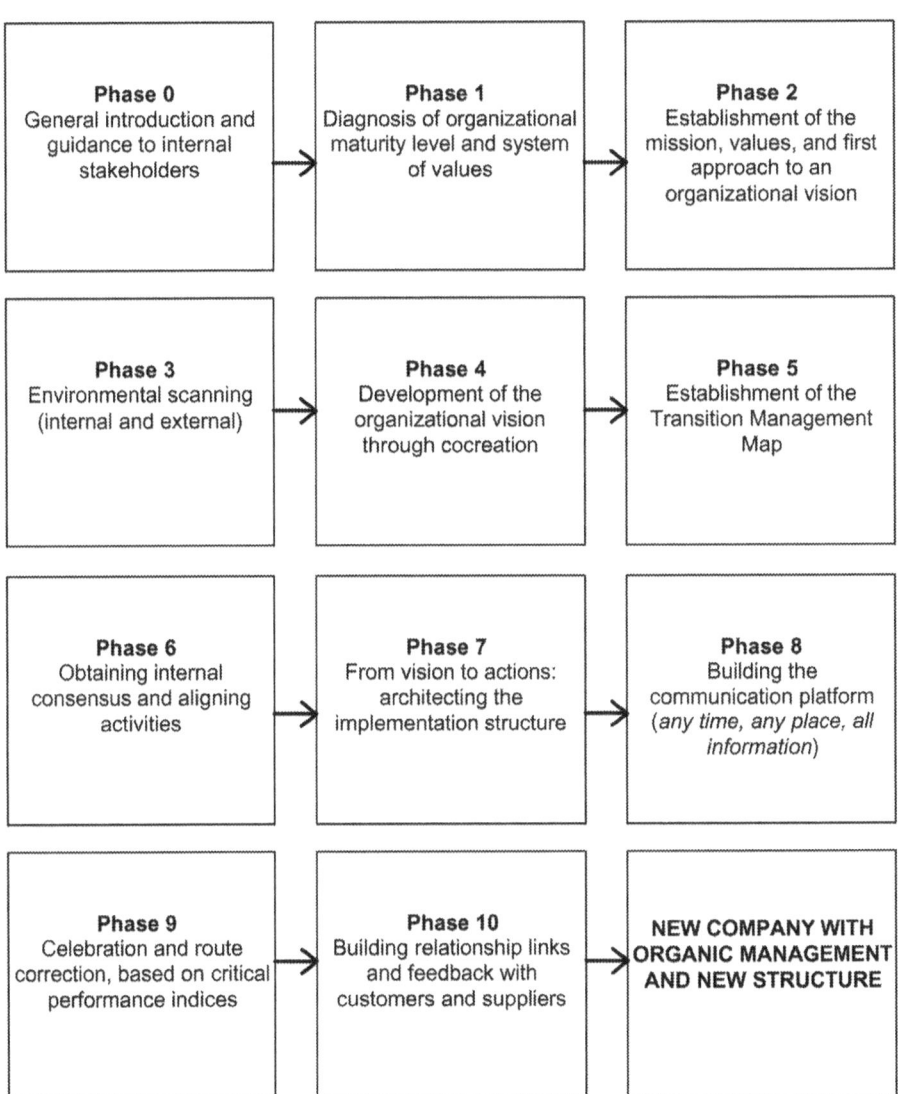

This is how the transformation occurred with one of our Brazilian clients, Sintofarma, a pharmaceutical laboratory. We used a different sequence at other clients, in each case respecting their own individuality.

One way or another, every part of the company develops and strengthens each of the seven essential competencies. To develop the seven essential competencies fully, we transfer the tools used for the transformation to internal stakeholders from the start. Because the stakeholders have the tools and know how to apply them, the organic values system becomes a reality, not a mere promise for the future!

After a short period, rarely more than one or two years, even in more complex cases, the company integrates its management model with the improvements. From that point, the company can continue its own organic renewal, eventually extending the benefits of the change to its community and external stakeholders.

As I have already stressed, corporate cultures are usually conservative when it comes to change—in fact, all cultures are. To allow the transformation to advance until all those involved commit to its consolidation, the transformation team must neutralize the culture suck. As I mentioned earlier, a protected internal environment (a separate time and place) is essential for a new healthy organizational structure to develop.

It is the duty of top management to select high-caliber people from each division to form the team in charge of first steps of the transformation. These professionals, shareholders, and employees will be the pioneers in charge of the transformation, which means that high management must give them total decision-making autonomy and implementation powers. Only then will the results spread throughout the organization.

This reminds me of a case in which an early management and monitoring group of only five top executives grew during the transformation to a group of twenty-eight people from throughout the organization. In the end, the implementation team consisted of individuals who had struggled to reach the top of the company. At first, they strongly resented top management for treating them as creatures, but soon everyone was pulling together toward the corporate vision as equals, and reaching the top no longer mattered.

As the process progressed, it involved an increasing number of internal stakeholders, eventually several hundred. Management came to see that the rank-and-file employees were able to grasp the company's complex fundamental decisions, and this increased mutual trust.

An Improved Management Opportunity

Once top management has decided to carry out the organizational transformation project, the key executives must understand the depth of the coming transformation. Instead of simply trying to adjust or improve existing processes, the company will gradually regenerate itself, at a fundamental level. The organization as an organic whole will strive for what its members have identified as its best possible future, having considered its identity, values, and purpose, as well as its history, objectives, structure, and market.

The early outcome of this intervention is a feeling of trust among internal stakeholders, because they are now the active creators of a new and promising future for the organization and for themselves. They learn the principles that bring about organizational transformation: changes in attitudes, organic versus hierarchical structures, the stages of maturity, advancing from creature to creator, the S-curve, the seven essential competencies. They set up a common vocabulary for the process and main organizational features on which they will work. They take part in discussions that focus on ideas such as individual growth, personal or corporate patterns, and creator/creature profiles. They learn to use organizational tools, such as the corporate vision, essential competencies, and optimal organization. The company's members gain confidence that their efforts will be successful. As creators of their organization's future rather than creatures of fate (or top management), they now understand the steps necessary to design new ways for dealing with competition, diversity, and change.

Often, early in the transformation process the organization sees a generalized lack of confidence in its eventual success. Not only do the rank-and-file participants show doubt, but even top management shows misgiving and resistance, even when they are provided with special coaching. This happens because the participants are still at the opportunistic and conformist stages of personal maturity. People at these stages prefer that their managers tell them what to do, and they identify any change by its risks. Holding on to their hierarchical values system, few of them have experience working as a team. Managers give orders, and their subordinates carry them out mechanically. They now face the challenge of having to treat others as equals—regardless of their hierarchical position—in the diagnosis, analysis, and decision-making meetings to come. Although at first this might be threatening to some, it eventually becomes a rich experience for everyone and is the only valid way for the company to integrate the Seven Cs into its culture.

Consideration of some of the behavior characteristics relevant to the opportunistic and conformist stages of maturity is noteworthy here (because people at the impulsive stage rarely assume management positions in large organizations, considering their obvious immaturity and excessively egocentric attitudes).

Opportunistic individuals admit the existence of rules but only adopt them if they get immediate benefits; such is their concern with control, advantage, and domination. Thus, they exploit and manipulate people. This explains their difficulty in nurturing committed, cocreative, and confident relationships.

Conformist individuals, on the other hand, internalize rules but desperately seek acceptance and approval, evaluating others based only on accomplishment. Thus, their motivators are the tasks set by their superiors or referenced by their equals, and they have difficulty assuming a creative and innovative attitude.

The people in both these stages (most of them) will only be useful to the organizational transformation if the agents of transition skillfully and patiently help them become committed to their own evolution and to the organization's progress. People at the opportunistic stages are interested in better opportunities for themselves. Conformists see the organizational transformation project as a higher decision taken by the company and thus a chance to fit in.

Thus, in one fashion or another, everyone gradually learns to perform at a higher maturity level, to his or her personal benefit as well as the organization's benefit.

Regardless of the intervention model used and eventual adjustments made, what matters in this early phase is that the transition team clearly communicates the purpose and the rules that allow renewal (already accepted by high management) to everyone involved. Of course, it is equally important that the participants clearly understand them, too. This communication and understanding is the method for reaching a collective agreement. It simultaneously attenuates resistance, reaffirms transparency, and sets the foundation for personal and collective commitment to the proposed objectives.

From this point onward, the entire organization will be continuously learning and training to perform as a team. Internal stakeholders experience complete learning cycles (Kolb, 1976) through carefully planned tasks, as shown in Figure 9. In this way, everyone gets to practice the Seven Cs in a conceptual, experimental, emotional, and intuitive way. This also gives stakeholders the opportunity to think about the organization and its environment, opportunities, threats, methods, processes, and products leading to proper action.

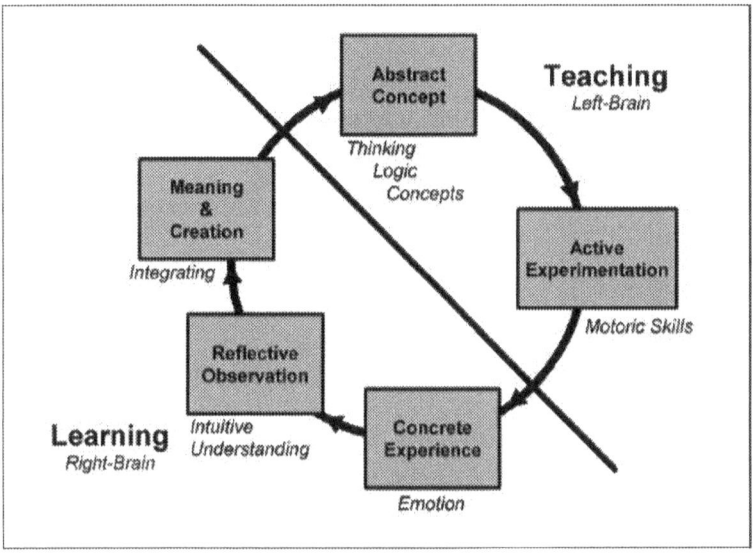

Figure 9: The learning cycle.

Preliminary Diagnosis of the Company

Parallel to this educational phase, it is important for the organization to understand where they are (current reality) and how far they are from their ideal state. They must understand how strong each of the Seven Cs is in the company, to help them decide which intervention model will be the most successful.

The focus at this point is not on identifying or measuring production, management, or business processes that need improvement. Rather, we concentrate on measuring the extent to which the company practices the essential competencies and the maturity of the organization's internal stakeholders (according to Loevinger's stages of ego development).

Table 5 is typical of a tool that we might use to assess the company's current reality.

Table 5: An Example of an Organizational Current Reality
Assessment Tool

Current Reality Assessment Tool

Competence 1—Confidence

- Do the members of the organization feel that they are creators of the future rather than inheritors of the past?

- Is there an overall feeling the organization can deal with any challenge it might face?

- Is there a clear organizational direction shared by its members?

- Do new employees quickly gain the knowledge and skills that they need to become productive?

- Do employees gain the training and information that they need to achieve their part of the vision?

- Is employee training and development linked directly to the corporate vision?

Competence 2—Commitment

- To what extent is the organization on purpose? That is, does it have a clear, understandable, and exciting corporate vision that it actively uses as a guiding light to stay on course into the future?

- Do the members of the organization readily identify with the company's identity, values, and purpose?

- Do the members of the organization feel proud of belonging to the company?

- Is the organization's purpose based on the specific needs of its customers, providing a framework for effective customer relations?

- Is customer communication an important part of the organization's strategic existence?

Competence 3—Cocreation

- Are the organization's members actively creating the future together?

- Does the organization have a corporate vision that offers a clear, comprehensive picture of what life will be like in the company on a certain day in the future?

- Does the corporate vision statement represent the future implementation of the organization's identity, purpose, and values, based on awareness of future trends in the business environment, and designed to satisfy the current needs of customers?

- Does the corporate vision lead the organization, and is everyone striving to achieve that vision?

Competence 4—Connection

- Is there an elegant interface between people and information systems that helps work become as effortless as possible?

- Are the organization's members skilled at converting current reality into the goals and tasks that continuously move it toward the corporate vision?

- Do the organization's members clearly understand the steps needed to fulfill the corporate vision?

- Can the organization's members establish a clear distinction between the time and space in which to manage today, and the time and space in which to structure the future?

- Do the task teams have the authority they need to put in place new business processes and workflows?

Competence 5—Communication

- Do the organization's members communicate effectively and enjoy communicating?

- Is everyone aware of the individual and collective progress toward the vision?

- Do the organization's members understand what communication they need to support the business processes essential to the vision, and have they fully developed that structure?

- Does the organization have an open communications system, manual or electronic, that enables the organization to coordinate and spread information quickly and effectively and keeps everyone apprised of how all tasks are progressing?

- Do the organization's members understand that communication technology is more than electronics, because it combines scientific principles and knowledge that apply to any human behavior?

Competence 6—Celebration and Course Correction

- Are there scorecards for each commitment, with specific details, milestones, and goals?

- Does the organization support a climate in which they celebrate successes, take risks in a mature way, and welcome course-correcting input?

- Does the organization have a system that identifies—and brings to suitable attention—exceptional performance and undesirable performance, based on purpose, values, vision, and customer input?

- Does the organization encourage employees to give feedback and direction to others in an open and positive manner?

Competence 7—Caring and Crossing

- Is there a prevailing atmosphere of caring in the organization—for customers, suppliers, colleagues, products, tools, and facilities?

- Does a general feeling of mutual respect and trust exist? Does it go beyond the organization's boundaries to include everyone with whom the organization interacts?

- Does the organization have a system that allows a continuous back-and-forth flow of information with customers or suppliers?

Understanding the organization's current reality in detail is crucial. Companies whose internal stakeholders are largely less mature have less developed essential competencies and need a different intervention than organizations with more mature employees. Because so many companies have hierarchical values systems, and because this system causes a decline in adaptability, productivity, and profitability, most stakeholders perform at low maturity levels. Any efforts that develop these competencies and help the organization's stakeholders to mature will benefit the organization in both the short- and the long-term.

It is also important to define the values that govern the organization, because the interaction between the purpose and values defines the identity. People and organizations that have developed a sense of identity are more centered and feel more in control. They are more competent to deal with changes in customers, market, and community. In addition, an integrated sense of identity produces powerful unity in efforts and actions, allowing the organization to be proactive and flexible, emanating confidence, consistency, and accessibility.

Organizations with an integrated sense of identity have a clear sense of their potential and limits. They undertake actions that are in harmony with their identity. This allows them to achieve their objectives efficiently and profitably, without the negative emotions and frustration normally associated with actions that are inconsistent with the identity.

Further still, they understand the importance of interdependence, that is, creating a web of egalitarian relations that involves all internal stakeholders. Treated as valuable assets by the organization, the stakeholders will develop and continuously adapt the structure, products, and processes that affect their corporate life.

Are We Who We Think We Are?

The outcome of this is a preliminary vision based on the personal values, purpose, knowledge, and experience of each of the company's main internal stakeholders, whether shareholders or contracted executives. It is reasonable to suppose that no one knows and shares the organization's purpose, values, and identity as much as this group. It is important, however, to identify which parts of the vision have to do with an idealized corporate image (what the company thinks it is) and which parts represent the organization's current reality.

In psychodynamic terms, the organization must distinguish the idealized self-image from the behavior practiced in the company. Imagine a company that considers itself democratic and participative, although it reserves an exclusive elevator for shareholders and directors and does not allow certain hierarchical levels to dine in the same lunchroom. The action plan to deal with this inconsistency could be something like the following:

- Help top management to define or affirm the corporate purpose, based on the company's identity and values;

- Help them align the organizational values with their own by starting to distinguish between those the company merely imagines and those it practices effectively;

- Convert the purpose and values into daily behaviors;

- Create a program to reinforce behaviors that are congruent to the purpose and values and to redirect the behaviors that violate these;

- Produce guidance material, both internally and externally.

For an organization to maintain a genuine picture of its current reality, it must continually scan its environment. Such *environmental scans* encompass the company's internal and external environment and evaluate the company's actual behavior with respect to its identity, values, and purpose. The result is a "scanning way of life," a continuous discovering of all opporthreats to a particular organization. As we said earlier, the word *opporthreat* implies that any opportunity inherently contains a related element of threat, just as every threat contains a seed of opportunity. A thorough understanding of the opporthreats serve as a basis for a final version of the company's statements of identity, values, purpose, and vision that are as close to the current reality as possible.

A complete environmental scan looks for trends in at least six areas:

1. Economic

2. Environmental

3. Political

4. Regulatory

5. Social

6. Technological

Only by examining all six types can an organization gain a true picture of its overall environment. It is also important that representatives of all areas of the organization are involved in these scans. Each area of specialty will have its own interpretation of each trend and will add valuable insight to each. A proper environmental scanning system has the following characteristics:

- Uses cross-cultural scanning teams

- Collects, classifies, categorizes, and saves facts, trends, events, news items, statistics, and qualitative information

- Analyzes data for direct or indirect pertinence to the organization

- Draws conclusions, categorized into opportunities and threats

- Distributes pertinent information to all interested parties in the company

My colleagues and I have noted over the years that this multidisciplinary approach can be a source of disagreement and conflict. People in a power hierarchy take it for granted that a specialist from one area should not systematically offer contributions to other power structures within the organization. This, in turn, restricts company members' performance possibilities and may even induce among internal stakeholders a lack of commitment toward their equals. This condition often results in a shortsighted company unable to see different facets of reality.

The central objective of multidisciplinary scanning is to allow internal stakeholders from all company areas to interact together and take part in tasks that contribute to the continuous renewal of the organization, regardless of their specialty or hierarchical position. They cause internal knowledge exchange (which alone would be a great achievement considering the fragmented nature of most organizations). This leads to positive democratic dealing and organic performance from the outset of the transformation process, opening interdepartmental barriers, satisfying individual safety and acceptance needs, helping all stakeholders to mature, and producing a more flexible company. These activities concurrently lead to greater trust among participants, reaffirming their commitment to the company while developing the skills necessary for continuous multidisciplinary scanning. The entire organization learns to advance in this way, rather than leaving it up to the research department alone.

The result of the scanning is more important than the information that the teams gathered, or even the quality of the analyses that they produced—which they can always revise or expand later. The true benefit is that internal stake-holders start to use a new behavior model that is healthier and more reward-ing. From this point on, the company's organic values and effective needs are the ones that dictate the company's management model, supported by the continuous exercise of the essential competencies.

Company Self-Diagnosis

Experienced professionals now have to abandon their rigid power hierarchies, functional segregation, and activities predetermined by organization charts. These conditions expose the lack of creativity, flexibility, adaptability, and self-esteem that exists in themselves and the company. Executives who nor-mally raise matters only within their scope of action now have to discuss mat-ters relevant to other specific areas. They have to consider issues that are of general interest, such as macroeconomic matters, legal trends, technology, or personnel management. In addition, they now must interact with people in other levels and areas of the company as equals. This in principle makes them feel uneasy.

Everyone has their own opinions about the other areas in the organization with which they have contact. However, they normally limit conversations with these "outsiders" to subjects specific to their own field or comfort zone. Although this behavior gives them greater feelings of control, it freezes the com-pany's internal knowledge flow, sapping much of its potential for flexibility.

As the organization grows to become a large, complex company, the infor-mation flow becomes bureaucratic and thus even more rigid, with equally slow responses and sluggish practices. This is because the individuals who manage the flow of knowledge are normally opportunistic or conformist professionals. They have strong hierarchical values that motivate them toward power or a specific role in the hierarchy. Their values system causes them to adopt mech-anistic rituals and dualistic notions (black versus white, good versus bad, right versus wrong). They become the deadwood of the organization, helping to reduce productivity, de-energizing others, and sapping profitability.

In practice, multidisciplinary environmental scans reveal to everyone the vast confident richness offered by shared knowledge and mutual learning. They do this without diluting or discounting the expertise of the people involved. For example, imagine a stakeholder from the production division confidently taking part in the group that is analyzing technological trends, offering significant contributions to his colleague from the finance department. Similarly, both will learn from their colleagues in the marketing or sales departments, especially if they are involved in scanning market conditions.

The protected atmosphere of the transition effort allows trust and openness gradually to replace the early feelings of distrust and self-protection. Shareholders and employees feel free to express their opinions about each specific characteristic of the company. All areas get to know one another better.

Simultaneously, scanning the company's current reality reveals discontinuity between the identity, values, and purpose and its current practices. Often, tools such as Corporate Transitions' *Anthropologic Study of Values* reveal that the values upheld by the company are incompatible with its daily routine. This situation always results in conflicts, frustration, resentment, and low productivity.

Understanding the discontinuities between the desired outcome and current reality also helps to identify the best methodology for corrective intervention. As internal stakeholders become aware of the company's strengths and weaknesses in all areas, they can better target improvements.

Because behavior patterns are deeply rooted in the stakeholders' emotional structures, they strenuously resist unmasking and redirecting them. Frequent group meetings significantly contribute toward success and individual maturity. Participants begin to substitute new habits and attitudes for old ones, and their self-confidence increases. Remember, three are happening in parallel: (1) The environmental scanning is one step in the process that is moving the organization towards the vision. (2) The process is simultaneously strengthening each of the Seven Cs. (3) Because the stakeholders are working together in more mature ways and are overcoming difficult and important challenges, they are becoming more mature. This entire process must occur carefully and gently because of personal resistance and variations in individual rhythms.

Overcoming resistance needs trust, and connected cocreation respects the individual and causes trust. Celebration of results and course correction reaffirm commitment, stress care, and intensify communication in the tasks that drive internal stakeholders. This helps them to mature.

Meanwhile, the integrators in charge of coordinating the project provide the coaching to promote teamwork. Regular assessment meetings soften resistance, facilitate discussions, and preserve the focus. General working rules help redirect activities whenever necessary.

This is how the organization builds its new dynamic structure: step by step. It uses the best of the old structure and its own knowledge capital, financial capital, and human capital. The company's essential competencies bloom. The new dynamic helps all members harmoniously engage in diagnosis and creating solutions for the organization. Each individual's success becomes part of the team's success, and mistakes become learning opportunities.

The information gained through environmental scans and the resultant conclusions is ultimately available to everyone. It will form an organized base of collective knowledge about the company's business environment and trends. Therefore, everyone can have an overall picture of the company's main production, management, and commercial processes.

We have found that it is essential for the members of the company to have, from the outset, a solid connection with the current reality (internal and external). The environmental scans, when properly communicated throughout the organization, help achieve this.

One of the most important steps of organizational transformation occurs after the scanning teams complete their environmental scans. They revise them and communicate them to the stakeholders, giving the company a clear connection to its current reality. Now the organization is ready to cocreate its corporate vision.

Chapter 7

Consolidating the Re-creation for Survivability

In the last chapter, you saw how a company must perform self-diagnosis in order to understand its current reality. This is an indispensable basis for creating the corporate strategy and connecting with the future. In this chapter, I will show the steps necessary to create the corporate strategy.

A Vision for a Better Future

Put in the simplest terms, the corporate vision is a projection of the organization's identity, purpose, and values. Several factors—including stakeholders' needs, internal structures, and trends in the business environment—interact to form its basis. It is always specific to the company under consideration, because the company itself cocreates it.

However, the corporate vision must be more than just a collection of wishes. It must be a clear statement of sincere intent, to which everyone in the company can commit. In other words, it must proudly depict the exciting and compelling future of the organization. It must show in elegant detail the grand cathedral that all stakeholders will be carrying stones to build. It is through the vision that the "Thank God it's Friday" syndrome becomes "Wow! It's Monday!"

Before the entire organization cocreates its shared vision, the existing management team should develop a seminal vision based on their personal visions. This is an important moment, a template for the entire organizational transformation process. The leaders go through a specific process to arrive at the vision. They first fashion their personal vision of the company in five or ten years in the future. They use a combination of their specialized knowledge and their personal psychological profile. They include the company's current reality, the environmental trends, its values, its purpose, and its identity. Then they bring their personal vision for the company into discussions that will eventually lead to a single corporate vision statement. In these discussions, they collect all the strong points from each individual vision and discard the weak. There is no room for delay, playing tricks, setting up opportunist alliances, or adopting conformist behaviors.

Through a fearless act of cocreation in an environment of confidence, committed and connected to its current reality and future trends, the leaders of the organization create the initial vision. This will act as a framework to guide the company into the future. It is faithful to the values, identity, and purpose, all reaffirmed during the discussions leading up to its cocreation. The process takes advantage of the mass of intelligence, knowledge, and experience brought together to analyze the vision exhaustively and thus confirm its validity. The outcome is a document that reflects the leaders' desired future for the organization. This vision (or most likely a descendant), as you shall see in the next chapter, will soon be shared by everyone in the organization. It will eventually permeate all the company's decisions, and become a full-time counselor for effective decision making and strategic guidance.

The most important effect of this initial vision on the organization, however, is greater than a long-term improvement in decision making. *The revolutionary aspect of this vision is that from this point forward, the company's top managers recognize the corporate vision as their leader, rather than any person or group.* The corporate vision now guides all top-level decision making, uniting their efforts to achieve shared objectives within a specific period. The leaders' thinking begins to be long-term rather than immediate, strategic rather than tactical. The leaders start to work, analyze, produce, and make decisions in an organic and participative manner. The organization sets forth on a new, more successful course.

Another result of the initial vision is that the process strengthens the Seven Cs in top management, adding flexibility and vigor to the organization. Because the method used to create the vision depends upon these competencies, it cultivates them and encourages behaviors aligned with them.

It also plants the seeds for continual renewal of the vision through analysis and consensus. The environment in which an organization lives (customer needs, organizational abilities, and market trends) is continually changing, so the basis of the vision (but not necessarily the purpose or values) must shift correspondingly. In keeping with the Seven Cs and the principles of Organizational Architecture, such changes must result from the broadest stakeholder consensus possible, as I shall explain in detail later in this chapter.

Corporate visions like the ones discussed—collectively created, and considering the company's internal and external environment—become the true leaders of organic, learning organizations. They provide for continual and fruitful renewal, responding to the needs of all stakeholders. Through this effort, the leaders begin to substitute organic values for hierarchical ones. They have made clear the type of organization that they want and to which they are committed.

The company is now ready to cocreate a corporation-wide vision. This broader vision, like the initial vision, is an outgrowth of its purpose and values. The key difference is that all internal stakeholders, not just top management, will share it. It will build confidence, willingness to change, resilience, interdependence, integration, and maturity throughout the organization. It will improve the company's ability to take advantage of opportunities or face challenges as a team.

A shared, cocreated vision helps every stakeholder align with the organization's purpose and act according to its values. It makes these actions efficient and orderly, and helps the organization optimize the use of its available resources. The corporate vision, when shared and understood at every level and division of the organization, ensures that the organization has a strong, clear identity (as defined in Chapter 2). Because the identity is so strong, everyone pulls together to achieve the corporate vision. Because they understand the organization's strategy, stakeholders are free to be more creative in their own actions, according to their personal abilities and the tasks that are theirs. Creativity leads to success, which increases individual and organizational maturity, thus increasing the stakeholders' commitment to the organization and motivation to succeed, while cutting out the organization's less productive pieces.

To gain these new attitudes, it is essential for internal stakeholders to cocreate their strategy, increasing commitment at all levels of the company. It is also important, if possible, to extend the cocreation to stakeholders outside the company (as much as is possible at the current stage of development). This process requires a precise definition of its identity, values, purpose, and vision.

Consolidating the Purpose

Ideally, every decision and action taken by the organization is in alignment with its purpose. However, when a clear, noble definition of the organizational purpose is lacking, most people make decisions based on their personal purpose. This leads to scattered, unintegrated, seemingly random behavior from the organization. It has an obviously negative effect on the organization's ability to keep employees and customers or to compete—much less sail a tsunami.

If the organization's purpose is noble, people feel that they are doing something important. In fact, the nobler the organization's purpose, the greater the motivation for people to work as a team. This produces an intense feeling of being part of a community. One paper recycling company, for example, thought that its purpose was to make money out of used paper. Through Organizational Architecture, the company realized that it was saving trees, preserving forests, and protecting humanity. This boosted its morale and reenergized the organization.

Another company was in the business of making microchips to monitor vibrations in airplanes. Organizational Architecture revealed that the company's purpose was "to expand human ability of sensing otherwise imperceptible vibrations, thus protecting human lives from the undesirable outcomes such vibrations could produce." As well as expanding the company's scope beyond commercial aviation, this electrified a sales force that suddenly realized they were saving lives, radically altering their perception of their mission.

On the other hand, some companies affirm that their purpose is "to consistently produce profits," which we refer to as the "bottom-line syndrome." Selling and making profits is fundamental to success, but profit by itself is a false purpose. Following Maslow's scale of values, financial stability is one of humanity's primary needs, which comes well before the more mature needs of self-accomplishment. A purpose centered on profits is therefore not likely to hold onto the more mature personalities, and it shows nothing for the customers and the community to admire! This is why it is so important for an organization to have a noble purpose.

In cases where the company has not defined its purpose, exploring the founders' reasons for starting the company may be a good start. In most cases, founders clearly realize what they want to achieve through the company beyond selling and making profits. This is why the founder's original perspective merits rediscovery and careful analysis, even if the market and environment has imposed changes or the stakeholders' needs have shifted over time. In general, there is a noble purpose behind the company's original perspective.

If people sense alignment between the company's purpose and their personal, family and community values, the organization will attract them like a magnet. They will become committed to it, whether as a customer, investor, or employee. Otherwise, stakeholders will constantly question the company's identity and its integrity. Furthermore, consider the influence that companies have on people outside of work and thus their communities. Noble organizational purposes will help to shape noble purposes in society.

However, even a clear, noble purpose will not help the organization become more organic unless cocreated by all the stakeholders, shared throughout the organization, and used by everyone as a basis for decisions. Only organic organizations (who are therefore agile, adaptable, and resilient) can survive a tsunami.

The Strategic Role of Values

The organization's values system also guides the decisions (and thus the actions) of all internal stakeholders. In addition, the values statement tells the external stakeholders what behavior to expect.

Values relate directly to integrity. Recent popular vernacular defines integrity as "talking the talk and walking the walk." Integrity has the same Latin root as the word *integration*, so we say that integrity is "integrating actions with values." For example, if a person who publicly promotes family values is caught having an affair, he or she is not acting with integrity. A company that espouses a strong environmental stance while polluting rivers shows a clear lack of integrity. On the other hand, a company that has taken the value "excellent customer service" and used it to make each customer contact a delightful experience is acting with integrity.

However, an organization cannot have integrity without clearly understanding and establishing its values system. Unfortunately, people and organizations rarely focus on their true values. They prefer to act in a confused and unpredictable way, according to the feelings of the moment, cultural truisms, or intuition. This behavior is far easier than undertaking a courageous, systematic analysis of what they believe and then acting in accordance with those beliefs. The result of this haphazard decision making is undependable behavior resulting in disloyalty from and among internal and external stakeholders. The organization is constantly acting against itself, compromising its image, integrity, and profitability. Decisions taken without this solid backing normally lead to failure.

Decisions based on the values demonstrate integrity. Behaviors aligned with the values strengthen the organization's identity, just as actions contrary to its values weaken it. Because a strong identity is essential to success, integrity is indispensable. The following values statement of a large retail chain is a good example, and shows the conciseness and clarity a values statement should have:

"We believe in:

- Mutual respect and caring for individuals and the organization,

- In preserving transparency and loyalty,

- Valuing people for their competence and commitment,

- The coresponsibility for developing the potential of people,

- The importance of the profitability of our business,

- Agile and participative structures,

- Simplicity, enthusiasm and belief in the future,

- Information Technology as a tool for the company's structuring and innovation,

- The commitment towards satisfying customer needs, always offering them the best cost-benefit relation possible,

- The value of keeping pace with innovations and a strong presence in the market,

- In human beings as creators."

However, merely developing a clear set of values, especially if done only at the upper management level, is not enough. Everyone in the organization must make decisions and act based on the shared organizational values. This allows the company to work as a unified block—agile, flexible, and interdependent. Thus, the values must be in place and in use in every corner of the organization.

Creating the Shared Vision

As I said in Chapter 4, to achieve an organic organizational structure all internal stakeholders must feel the personal commitment that results from cocreating its strategy and structure. This can be difficult or impossible without large-group consensus methods such as Dannemiller-Tyson Associates' Whole-Scale sessions that I mentioned in Chapter 4. These allow the entire organization or a representative cross-section—hundreds or even thousands of stakeholders—to analyze, discuss, and define the strategy and structure then merge the results into a harmonious consensus.

Using Whole-Scale-type meetings, the organization as an integrated entity can adjust or reaffirm the purpose, and can review and revise the values. The whole organization can perform new, more comprehensive environmental scans. Either this reaffirms top management's preliminary vision statement or (more often) triggers cocreating changes and improvements to the vision.

As more and more of the layers in large corporations become involved in the transformation, the commitment increases. It becomes easy to identify those who are still living the "Thank God it's Friday" syndrome, individuals and groups who see the organization as merely a money-earning apparatus, who fulfill their personal purpose elsewhere.

Each corporate vision evokes a desired state for that company. At Yázigi-InterNexus, for example, the collective efforts of its internal stakeholders resulted in the following corporate vision:

- InterNexus is a worldwide chain of educational and cultural services, dedicated to developing the world's citizens. To do this, it promotes continuous learning experiences, which help people to interact with others in all parts of the world.

- InterNexus is a dynamic organization that is constantly changing and growing, aimed at offering unique opportunities for developing the profiles of their students and customers.

- Shared beliefs guide InterNexus offices and its people's actions, rather than the hierarchical command structure. To achieve this, it is controlled by a system of interrelated representative councils, with leaders' roles directed to qualifying and guiding rather than demanding or charging.

- InterNexus has a flexible and concise structure that alternates global performance with strong regional autonomy of its units, qualifying them to perform in their markets while respecting the particularities of the countries in which they are present.

- The entire InterNexus chain is managed by qualified leaders, dedicated to developing their units by spreading the corporate vision and strengthening its identity.

- The programs at InterNexus focus on all age groups and genders, stimulating autonomous learning and interactive activities between teachers and students using state-of-the-art technology and educational resources.

- InterNexus provides personalized support for teaching foreign languages, transcultural training and development of international business profiles, catering to institutions, companies, communities and countries.

- InterNexus continuously researches the global environment to discover new ways to help individuals to achieve their educational objectives.

- Backed by solid values firmly set up in all its units, InterNexus works with other organizations and companies to guarantee the highest possible quality of its programs and products, whether directly or through such partnerships.

- Furthermore, InterNexus also works to help people to be better citizens through social consciousness programs and voluntary activities embracing environmental issues, art and culture appreciation, since its highest objective is to promote the personal development of its customers.

- InterNexus develops and provides services and products that qualify people to learn languages and cultures, whether through traditional methods such as physical classes and printed publications or remote learning resources.

- These products and services are developed at InterNexus research centers, always using state-of-the-art resources aligned with its values, while providing intercultural experiences through coordinated trips and exchange programs linking all parts of the world.

- The InterNexus brand is disseminated through video communication designed to improve communication between its units and customers, and to satisfy public needs.

- InterNexus strives to assure mutually favorable relations with local governments and communities, including alliances with their organizations, thereby complementing its purpose.

- InterNexus strives to develop and offer products and services of the highest quality and is continuously searching for innovation, creating means that are constantly updated through its educational franchises.

- InterNexus customers are attended locally by the worldwide chain of franchised units, connected by the ideal of serving humanity using state-of-the-art technology.

- InterNexus continuously seeks involvement in humanitarian, social and environmental activities throughout the world, by mobilizing its network of members.

- Accurate personnel selection and ongoing training of employees assure the high quality of InterNexus products, services and management.

- Communications systems such as the Internet, videoconference and shared databases afford InterNexus with the ability of keeping a constant exchange of experience and knowledge.

- InterNexus assures friendly, cooperative and loyal working conditions to its employees, as well as preserving open ethical relations with its suppliers. This assures the best possible protection and return on shareholders' investments.

- InterNexus is an open company that offers bonus and stock options to its employees and shareholders, promoting intense participation and firm commitment of all members towards the organization.

- In every location where it is present, the InterNexus chain is founded by its franchise holders.

At Sintofarma, the internal stakeholders arrived at a more concise corporate vision:

- We are a modern organization endowed with high technology and a high degree of productive automation and flexibility.

- Our personnel structure is sufficient and qualified.

- We have a motivating social policy with strong interpersonal relationships.

- We are ecologically and socially concerned.

- We invest in integrated training programs.

- We have a strong institutional image.

- We uphold mutual cooperation agreements with scientific and technology research institutions.

- We are active in several market segments through our business units offering diversified products.

- Computer technology is used intensively making information available to everyone.

- We constantly conduct market research.

- We seek and are called to set up new partnerships.

- We outsource some of our activities.

- We have a clear and transparent understanding of the company's objectives.

- We respect the environment.

At Atlantic Packaging, the stakeholders came up with the following corporate vision:

- Atlantic Packaging a billion dollar corporation, supplies the North American market through its six paper and polypropylene plants, nine corrugated cardboard plants, three or more fine lining paper plants and three toilet paper and card paper plants to satisfy the needs of all other industrial units.

- We have distribution centers in several locations in North America that deliver our own products, as well as third-party products.

- Our Investment Division is endlessly seeking opportunities in our fields of expertise.

- Our plants and warehouses are strongly automated and managed by personnel that are intensely trained, motivated and dedicated.

- Our facilities and equipment are technically advanced, with instantaneous communication using computer technology. This connects consumers and suppliers, allowing instantaneous communications in all phases of our business processes.

- Operating Day-Care Centers and constant assessment and training of our employees attract and retain the best professionals.

- A President directs each major division.

- Our operating executives work independently from our administration executives.

- We have finally reached a stage in which our chief executives are no longer restricted to managing daily activities and can now focus their efforts on orchestrating the dynamic growth of our company.

From the Vision to Objectives and Actions

Once the company has a company-wide vision in place, it must decide on the actions to take to achieve it. After all, actions without a strategy are futile, just as a vision without action is just a dream. The organization must convert the vision into a series of precise strategic objectives, quantifying each statement in the vision. The quantity of strategic objectives may vary from one company to another, because of its current reality and the complexity of its vision statement.

Once the stakeholders have defined the objectives that lead to the company's vision, the whole mass of information must be organized and prioritized. This involves a rating system based on the relative importance of the objective to the overall effort and the extent to which the organization has already achieved it.

Regardless of the number of participants, the methodology provides an egalitarian environment. Processes and procedures ensure that everyone's opinion goes into the result, excluding or forgetting no one. Digital voting technology also improves the process by making the difficult prioritizing process quicker and less burdensome.

Having defined and prioritized the main objectives, the organization arrives at a general strategic map, resulting from internal stakeholders' experience, environmental scanning, and the corporate vision designed by all shareholders and employees.

At this point, the internal stakeholders should celebrate their achievements and assimilate the results of collective work. This pause is important because it strengthens commitment. Then they must once again go to work on the transformation.

The work to this point alone, that is, having a noble purpose, a clear vision statement, an exciting vision, and a set of challenging objectives would justify all the effort. However, if Organizational Architecture ended here, it would not differ much from several of the better models for creating organizational strategies. Many programs deliver good strategic planning with precise goals and critical performance indicators but lack the ability to create a mature, agile, organic organization. The uniqueness of Organizational Architecture is that it works in such a way that the stakeholders gain the business muscles that help them work with other stakeholders (internal and external) in a more mature way. This process builds the maturity, both personal and organizational, that is essential for survivability and tsunami-sailing skills.

At this point, the stakeholders go to work carrying out the strategy—creating the new organization that they had described in the previous stages. Their task is to suggest actions aimed at achieving the objectives necessary to fulfill the corporate vision fully within the desired period, using the resources available to the company (whenever possible).

Once again, the group that is involved in this part of the process should be a representative cross-section of the entire organization or in some cases *be* the entire organization. They will divide into multidisciplinary subgroups that represent all the company's functional areas to do the work. Their objective is to analyze alternatives and to recommend objective-oriented actions for each internal function (such as financial administration, communication, accounting, inventory control, distribution, personnel management, marketing, research and development, production, information technology, and sales).

After the subgroups finish discussing and analyzing actions, they come up with an action list. Meeting again as the whole group, they merge the proposals into a single *action list*, merging similar actions to keep focus. Then they prioritize the actions in a process similar to the one that they used on the objectives, that is, according to their importance of each action to achieving the vision and its current degree of achievement within the company.

Regardless of which actions are proposed or chosen, the process that they used to do so will cause the participants to reevaluate their notion of management structure and leadership. What's more, they reassess the importance of the company's assets, processes, and personnel with respect to the corporate vision. Thus, they become more organic in thought and attitude, adding maturity and increasing their value to the company and the company's overall worth.

In this way, the entire company matures, and its managers, shareholders, and employees develop more commitment. They become confident cocreators, connecting with reality, celebrating victories, and correcting mistakes, always with due care for the company and the other stakeholders.

We recently worked with a major newspaper to help it become more organic and mature. The way the newspaper turned its vision into an action plan provides a good example of this process. The client, using the Organizational Architecture process and the Whole-Scale methodology previously described, created the following corporate vision for five years in the future:

> The newspaper has consolidated its brand name in national communications and is recognized nationally and internationally as the largest and most influential newspaper in the country.
>
> Its above average economic and financial results in its market, combined with its credibility, solidity, and integrity attract readers and advertisers. This results from its traditional journalistic ability to inform, mold and influence private initiative, promoting democratic liberties, human rights, and citizenship in an ethical, analytical, and democratic manner.
>
> It is the leader in national circulation for its strategic market, especially in the state capital and the interior.
>
> Recognized as a modern communications medium, it is respected and preferred by the public in general.
>
> Significantly present in the main capitals and cities of the nation, it stands out as a newspaper that offers social, economic and political information and analysis. Thus, it detects trends and helps interpret cultural and economic changes in society and other facts that influence the daily activities of its readers.
>
> Its solid information sources put it in a leading position in the supply of editorial and commercial content for various media.
>
> The newspaper's intense concern with culture, education, and the environment produces material that is used as an educational reference by a public interested in research and social development.

It is the most technologically-advanced newspaper in the country, and one of the most modern in the world.

Capable of anticipating changes imposed by technology—especially regarding new media and their application—it continuously maintains and improves the profitability of its operations, assuring satisfactory returns on shareholder investments and the funding necessary for the investment programs that insure its continued success.

The proactive and creative development of communication solutions anticipates the needs of a diversified market, offering distinguished editorial products to address local, regional, or national needs, specific to the region covered and theme of interest.

All this, plus constant investments in the quality of its products, leads to market preference for the newspaper, its analyses, and its advertising services, guaranteeing the prestige of its brand and repeat advertisement sales.

Our employees are motivated to succeed, and the company has the ability to attract, identify, develop, and retain qualified professionals that "make a difference," and who are committed to the ethical and professional values that are recognized and defended by the company.

Our contributors are well paid, and their commitment and results valued in an atmosphere that favors professional and personal development. This makes the newspaper one of the best companies to work for in the country.

With an advanced technological platform that allows it to be the most complete news media in the market, the newspaper is open to commercial, business and operational relationships, especially with organizations that have values similar to its own.

In this way, it continues to be of benefit to the most important group of communications companies in the country, funding new businesses which generate further success, making its 130 years of existence and leadership a matter of reaffirmed pride.

After the newspaper's management approved this cocreated corporate vision, internal stakeholders condensed it, in successive analysis and discussion sessions, into a statement with six major strategic assertions, or "Major Inspiring Objectives" as they called them. This statement was:

(1) To be recognized as the most important and influent newspaper in the country and
(2) To guarantee profitability requires
(3) Developing the best product for readers and advertisers,
(4) Continuously expanding our readership, and consequently
(5) Retaining the best talents in the national newspaper market,
(6) Using the best technology available.

Each of these assertions led to clearly defined strategic objectives, which were then broken down into actions, with precise metrics (results and performance), an overall schedule, and the people or groups responsible for each action.

This resulted in a general strategic map, composed of the corporate vision, strategic objectives, and hundreds of different tasks that they plan to accomplish in five years.

Helping Companies to Mature

In Chapter 6, I wrote about Organizational Architecture's four goals. In this section, I would like to discuss further the fourth goal, "To help internal stakeholders advance from creatures of fate to creators of their own futures, strengthening their commitment towards the company."

When performing environmental scans, building the corporate vision and breaking it down into strategic objectives and actions, shareholders and employees gradually learn, individually and collectively, the Seven Cs. This allows them to satisfy increasingly higher personal needs, such as safety, social acceptance, self-affirmation, self-esteem, personal growth, and creative autonomy. In every task, stakeholders assess their threats (in search of safety) and evaluate their personal exposure (affirmation within the group). They consider the right moment to intervene in discussions (social acceptance), reveal their doubts while gathering information (self-development), and help define projects (creative autonomy). While improving internal processes, each stakeholder continuously re-creates and preserves his or her agility, responsiveness, and adaptive flexibility through continuous learning and strong commitment toward positive results internally. This moves them toward maturity according to each individual's potential (as it improves the organization's overall maturity). All of this helps them to feel confident and empowered, because the company and their colleagues support them. Thanks to the prevailing atmosphere of trust and caring, they can now face collective challenges without feeling threatened.

My experience has shown that this type of intervention helps shareholders and employees to advance from opportunistic or conformist ego stages to the self-aware level, allowing them to advance from creatures to creators.

By carrying out the tasks in the way that we have described so far, the company will reinforce its own identity, values, and purpose. Obviously, there will be people in management who do not identify with the company the corporate vision projects. These will start showing their dissatisfaction in different ways. Some will be overt and vocal in their disapproval, and others will be covert, but the organization should be watching for this and must be aware of it when it happens. The transition team must identify these managers. Once identified, the team can counsel them, helping them analyze their personal purpose, values, and life goals, hopefully finding alignment between the company's vision and their own purpose. Without intervention, dissatisfied managers will naturally become alienated from the company and usually will begin to work against the transition program (culture suck). Unless the transition team can help them realign with the corporate vision, they will soon leave the company in a natural way, either voluntarily or through organic action of the other stakeholders. On the other hand, the managers who stay will have greater commitment to the identity, values, and purpose of the organization.

This deep commitment is the basis for their success and for that of the organization. Over and above anything else, advancing from creature to creator is what makes an individual or organization successful. Working on the transition helps all the stakeholders, not just the managers, do just that. The hierarchical values give way to an organic system, and the organization begins to realize its real profit in terms of increased creativity, productivity, and return on investment, plus the ability to preserve and increase all of these reliably.

The transition to higher ego stages is the result of the intense efforts and successful collaboration that take place as the stakeholders carry out the many tasks that lead to the vision. Through the transition process, they gradually discover and experience their true personal strengths. They will deal with personal resistances in an environment of trust that increases caring and in which they can commit more to the organization. Diversity and collective decision making is not as frightening as it used to be. They successfully deal with threats (satisfying their security needs), find out how much they can reveal their true selves to their teammates (thus satisfying their acceptance needs), express doubts, ask questions, and collect information (fulfilling their self-development needs). Finally, they propose initiatives and see them put into practice (satisfying their need to be creative).

Before the transition process, most managers, shareholders, and employees acted at an opportunistic or conformist level. My experience has shown that through this type of intervention, these individuals begin to operate at the self-aware level. This is the critical point where they start to view themselves as creators of their own destiny (and the organization's), rather than a creature of external powers. Few people reach the higher ego stages (autonomous or integrated), but by merely reaching the self-aware and conscientious stages, the whole organization takes a large step toward realizing its full potential.

The Transition Management Board and Mission Teams

The transition management board (TMB) is an embryonic model of the entrepreneurial and integrative functions that the organization will need to assure the creative management of its future and progress toward maturity. The TMB is a group with formal authority from the organization's leadership whose responsibility is to manage the entire transformation process. Most often the TMB *is* the organization's leadership. The TMB guarantees the implementation of a vision built by all stakeholders, thus integrating the organization with its strategy and diffusing confidence, commitment, mutual respect, and the other principles of integrated management throughout.

In practice, the TMB defines what is truly important from among the *strategic objectives* extracted from the vision. It decides what the organization needs to deal with first and what it can leave until later, because most organizations do not have the resources to do everything at once. The TMB's definition of priorities dictates a plan of action; on that basis, it chooses the *mission teams*, as will be discussed.

Once the mission teams are in operation, the TMB continually monitors and mentors their actions, course correcting and renegotiating their scope, resources, and so on as necessary. The TMB not only evaluates (through concrete metrics) their results, but it also ensures that the work of each team contributes to the integrated development of the organization as a whole. The successful interaction between TMB and teams will evolve into the new organic structure that the organization must have to thrive in this virtual age.

There is much work to do before the organization can move to these higher ego stages. It is impossible for the TMB to do it all themselves. Furthermore, even if the transition managers could do it, there would be no organizational growth. The only way forward is through mission teams, which will become the most precious internal resource of the company in its task of developing its own maturity muscles.

Mission teams are special cross-functional, cross-cultural, and cross-layer teams that the transition managers assemble to carry out the specific tasks called out in the action list. Mission teams use special procedures to fulfill their mission, and these procedures help them to build the muscles that they need for maturity.

Backed by effective information systems and caringly kept on course by the transition managers, mission teams help the organization rapidly achieve specific objectives. They design and set up new production or business processes and improve existing ones, always keeping in mind the strategies that are necessary to fulfill the vision.

It is not enough to involve only the managers and supervisors in the organizational transformation process, especially the development and cocreation of the vision and the strategic objectives. The process must involve every level, division, department, and functional area. Only by spreading the benefits from the process throughout the organization will it mature in an integrated way.

The transition champions must protect these special teams, just as in the early phases of the transformation process they protected the birth of the new organization. In the mission teams, the organization has to develop and nurture the activities that will take it to the corporate vision. This includes the growth of the new organic structure until it reaches the strength and health that it needs to exist throughout the organization.

To use the psychotherapy metaphor, the person and his or her facilitator decide the personality characteristics that they want to change, evaluate alternatives, and practice new behavior, always starting with the client's current reality. The person adopts new ways of being and behaviors in his or her daily environment (e.g., family, workplace, social clubs, emotional partnerships). In the therapist's office, the patient will evaluate the results week by week. The person will learn to monitor the process and make sure that all of his or her behaviors are in alignment with his or her purpose, values, and personal identity.

For the organization, the psychotherapy is the transformation process, and it also needs to follow the same steps, perfecting new processes and helping the stakeholders move on to higher stages of maturity, thus satisfying their maturity needs. The mission teams allow the organization to adopt the new management forms in a productive and protected way until all shareholders and employees are performing in the new organic mode. The success of the mission teams helps the organization gain the necessary competencies that it needs to achieve the vision.

To maximize the growth inherent in successfully completing their tasks, an organization should give the mission teams much independence. The transition management team encourages them to set their own goals, bounded by the organization's strategic objectives, plus it helps them set up the objectives, milestones, and budgets that they need to achieve the task successfully.

From this point forward, the company's renewal has started and the groups are working on perfecting the producing and administrative functions while integrating the entrepreneurial and integrative functions, as discussed in Chapter 5.

Obviously, I have described this complex process here in a simplified way, as if the company has decided to use this method of implementation throughout everything the organization does. In practice, has been shown that it is more prudent and productive to start this process with only a few teams carrying out tasks prioritized by their importance and the estimated success of implementation. On successful completion of their missions, the TMB breaks up the teams, and these veterans form the nuclei of other teams that will perform further important missions. The TMB will repeat this process until every employee is actively involved in moving the organization toward the vision. This is how the organization builds the new sailboat and learns to sail it through tsunamis.

Chapter 8

Good Communication to Integrate Efforts

In Chapter 4, I discussed the importance of the communication competency for an organization's survivability. In this chapter, I will show how to build an effective communication platform.

Every healthy and responsive organism depends on its senses to get data about everything that is happening in its internal or external environment. It then processes these data into information and possibly takes action in response. An organism constantly strives to restore equilibrium between itself and its environment. An organism in equilibrium can respond properly to every situation, whether to seize opportunities or deal with threats.

Ideally, an organization would be in equilibrium with its environment. At first, a company is. There is intensive information exchange throughout the organization. Almost everyone, shareholders or employees, knows what is going on. This increases the company's response speed and agility. However, as the company grows and creates new departments and hierarchical levels (differentiating roles and even displacing personnel to different locations), the lively flow of communication withers. The hierarchy replaces dynamic, organic activity with routines and procedures set forth in manuals, forms, standards, and bureaucratic decisions.

Most organizations structure themselves based on hierarchical values focused on rank and personal power. This structure shields management from the stakeholders. Gradually, the people in the organization develop a formal disinterest in other functional areas and start to defend departmental boundaries and possessions, including knowledge and information—the keys to good decisions. Over time, the organization as a whole becomes indecisive and unable to act in an effective and timely way.

Good Information Is Timely Information

If an organization wants to improve exchange of information (knowledge, ideas, objectives, and procedures) throughout the company, it needs to reorganize its communications structure. Note that this does not mean simply buying newer software, a different telephone system, or better computers. I am talking about a fundamental change in communication practices.

An uninhibited flow of information and decisions translates into a fundamental competitive advantage in this changing business environment. Opportunities arise and disappear as if by magic, uncovering threats and opportunities in unexpected market segments, and only those organizations with effective communication structures can respond quickly enough to take advantage of them.

In the past, when business environments changed slowly, badly informed managers and sluggish information flow were acceptable. There was always the excuse of preventing information leakage or being certain about the data. However, the rate of change in the marketplace is increasing, as is competition. This means that organizations must now develop the resources and procedures to give all internal stakeholders, in any place, at any time, the information necessary for making decisions that move the organization closer to the vision. This helps organizations become more responsive to environmental and internal changes, internally integrated, and agile.

Companies often need to relearn how to communicate, because for years or even decades they have relentlessly replaced effective communication with safe and largely ineffective practices. Companies are neither accustomed to a real-time, open flow of information within an organic structure nor are they willing to carry out the changes needed to bring this about. Besides, the less mature individuals resist open communication, even when necessary for healthy interdependence and productive integration. This explains why grapevine communication still prevails in companies, and is even more widespread in organizations that are less open structurally. As the formal communication paths become less and less useful, people improvise communication, and this is prone to error and misuse. Therefore, the company needs a new, effective communication protocol.

A good communication protocol involves all forms of interpersonal communication. Although many companies, especially in the last decade, have invested heavily in digital communication, this does not mean that they can communicate effectively. In fact, many companies have spent millions on digital systems, thinking that they were buying a silver bullet that would end their communications problems forever, only to find that their money was wasted and the systems poorly used.

Before the organization can use a cutting-edge communication platform, it must master the basics of communication. It is true that digital communication, such as e-mail, teleconferencing, knowledge management, workflow automation, electronic record keeping, and Electronic Data Interchange are an important part of the final picture. However, in an organization that has forgotten how to communicate effectively using *any* form of media, these tools only strengthen ineffective communication. The design and implementation of the communication platform must begin at the simplest level. It must begin with guidelines for two people exchanging information in a face-to-face conversation and protocols for paper letters and memoranda. From there, the organization can design structures around increasingly complex communication formats and media, such as meetings, presentations, telecommunication (fax and telephone), and mass media. Then it can use this as a basis for designing its digital information exchange and knowledge management. Only after everyone understands how to communicate effectively can all areas begin to exchange relevant information on a timely basis.

An effective communication protocol:

- Is easy to understand and to apply to any situation where two or more people need to communicate;

- Helps make every stakeholder decision and action more effective in terms of personal, team, and organizational strategy;

- Helps the TMB oversee and coordinate individual team activities and ensure their alignment and integration with the strategy;

- Allows the stakeholders to gather, store, retrieve, and exchange relevant data easily, thus reducing the need for meetings;

- Keeps everyone up to date about the current status of each task and its relationship with the strategic goals;

- Increases stakeholder interdependence, strengthening confidence, commitment, caring, and connection between individuals and teams;

- Sets up a virtual workplace that favors continuous cocreation;

- Allows the entire company to celebrate each successful achievement;

- Speeds up corrective feedback;

- Supports rapid course corrections;

- Reduces the incidence of informal information, so common in practice yet damaging to effective organic communication;

- Helps the organization build muscles by encouraging the constant, widespread use of all Seven Cs.

As the internal stakeholders learn to communicate effectively, they begin to exercise the Seven Cs. A new dynamic, agile, responsive, and continuously updated organic structure emerges and replaces the old hierarchical structure (as shown in Figure 10).

Note that the drawing on the left-hand side shows a hierarchical structure in which the information and decisions at the top must pass through several layers of gears to reach their destination at the bottom. One crank of the big wheel (upper management) makes all the little wheels spin like crazy, but the little wheels have almost no chance of making the big wheel move. In Figure 10, communication is free-flowing and interdependent, and everyone is working as an interconnected, integrated part of the whole to achieve the vision.

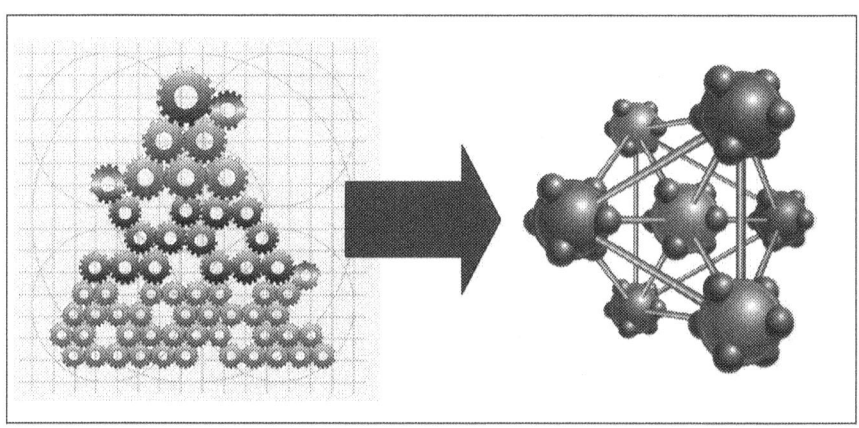

Figure 10: Transforming the structure from hierarchical to organic.

Obviously, while building this new organizational sailboat, the stakeholders will to various degrees resist the communications protocol and its implementation, as they resist most other changes. Because of their hierarchical value system based on control through reward and punishment, some will see this as just another way for the company to manipulate individual and collective performance. Others might fear information leakage, and a few more may say they find it difficult to use the new tools, preferring the old, reliable, printed forms and physical meetings.

The continued use of an effective communication protocol helps to consolidate the Seven Cs in the company, allowing it to become increasingly agile and competitive. This is a fundamental requirement, considering the current market environment.

Communication to Ensure Trust and Loyalty

Because they have the right communication tools, internal stakeholders experience growing confidence and easy information exchange. They rapidly lose their feeling of distrust and develop a proactive attitude. Their productivity increases. The communications platform becomes their virtual workplace. All internal stakeholders know the progress of every task, at any time and any place. The company starts to celebrate successes and correct off-course behavior at almost the moment they happen. The company's internal and external boundaries expand. Stakeholders—internal, external, and at all levels—increase their commitment to and participation in achieving the vision.

In fact, the communication platform makes possible continuing improvements, as all levels learn and practice the management practices used by the mission teams, as shown in Figures 11–14.

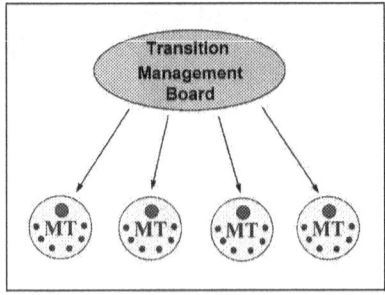

Figure 11: Early top-down communication from TMB to mission teams.

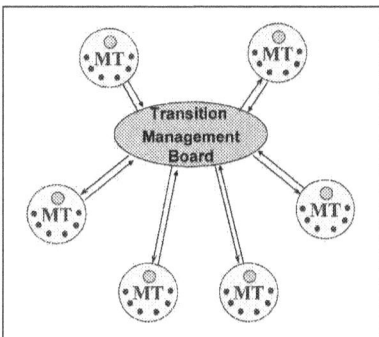

Figure 12: Advancement to dialog between TMB and mission teams.

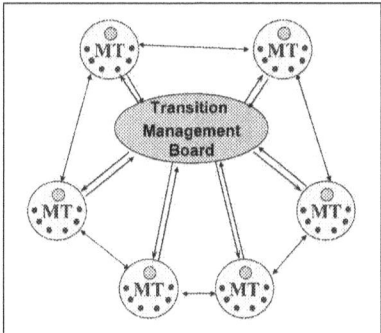

Figure 13: Adding effective communication among mission teams.

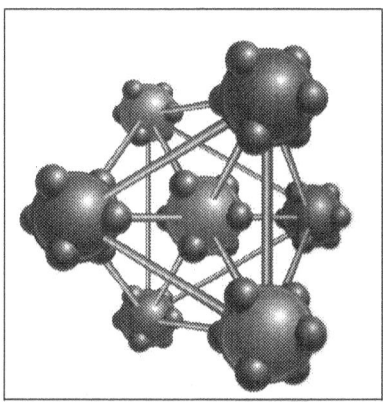

Figure 14: Total open communication.

This integration soon spreads throughout all the levels of the organization, eventually extending to customers and suppliers who are in contact with the company. Up to this point, most external stakeholders have not actively taken part in the process. They have perhaps briefly glimpsed this in the environmental scans, when the teams gathered information directly from suppliers or studied customer needs and characteristics. Now it is turning into a way of life.

Customers and Suppliers Make Good Partners

We are moving into a new business environment worldwide, worthy of a new human consciousness. This is what is behind all the new, previously unheard-of partnerships, associations, and business arrangements. Who, ten years ago, could imagine competitors joining efforts in an enterprise that is helpful to both? Who would have imagined a supplier who has direct access to one company's sales information while simultaneously selling to its competitors? Who could have foreseen a global company that no longer manufactures its products, dedicating itself instead to administrating its brand or supervising product distribution? Yet, all this is happening as I write this.

This new model, driven by higher stakeholder maturity, needs more openness and trust to achieve greater stakeholder loyalty (including suppliers and customers). Consumers in all markets are demanding increased quality and improved benefits from existing products and services. Environmental concerns create further pressure, also reflecting the evolution in human consciousness, rapidly changing consumer needs, demanding new products and services.

Expanding the Company's Boundaries

Companies are increasing marketing budgets to study behaviors, identify demands, define trends, and segment consumers, all to attract potential customers. They are also critically analyzing the return on their marketing investment. Still, only a few companies strategically manage supplier relations. Most still focus on getting the best quality for the lowest price, but this is no longer enough. Without supplier loyalty, companies cannot survive the tsunami.

When companies are starting up, they keep close relationships with suppliers, treating them almost as partners and sharing their needs and objectives. These confident and committed relations allow for quick communication and cocreation of processes and solutions. Over time, organizations traditionally come to distrust and distance themselves from their suppliers, losing the confidence and commitment that enabled these partnerships to be so effective.

To sail the organizational sailboat, the company will now have to face the challenge of restoring these valuable relationships. The extensive use of digital tools for contracting and managing suppliers (e-commerce) that started in the 1990s clearly helps this. We can see other important examples in growing business-to-business projects that partners manage virtually. Integrating the organization in a value-added production chain with its suppliers gives it the ability to control the entire process of satisfying the diverse needs of customers—which is always the company's purpose. More mature and ethical corporations will develop a deeper trust for each other.

The new communication protocol with its new tools (especially digital tools) introduces consistent, reliable strategic communication with business partners, customers, and the community. It also represents an important resource for building the organization's internal muscles and its new sailboat to survive the tsunami.

Summary

A company needs excellent communication to achieve and sustain success in the modern world, as trends over the past decade clearly signal. It is also the basis for expanding caring, trustful, and connected relations to customers and suppliers. Greater commitment and continuous cocreation, in a cycle of organic growth made possible by the never-ending practice of the Seven Cs, must become a way of life.

The company must share information rapidly and efficiently to ensure the satisfaction and well-being of its staff and to increase responsiveness, productivity, and profitability in the present and in the future. This is fundamental for forming and preparing leaders who can move beyond being creatures to become creators who will make the vision happen. These managers can help those that work with them to mature and develop their full productive potential, with benefits for the company, the stakeholders, and the community that supports them.

Chapter 9

New Leaders for a New World

In the last chapter, I stressed the importance of effective communication for surviving the tsunami. Equally important is the need for a new style of managerial leadership, not only to help build the organizational sailboat but to be able to use it in the turbulent waters ahead.

As I have said before, the new collective change in consciousness has created the need for a new business management model. Organizations must transform themselves, setting up not only a new, organic management model but also the new approach to leadership that this organic model demands. Such leaders will need new, more successful management techniques, as well as the ability to direct the tasks that will guarantee the survival of their organization in a constantly changing, increasingly demanding, and always challenging environment. Understanding this new leader will help us to see why conventional management models have offered little more than quick fixes for crumbling structures.

A Time of Transition

Table 6 summarizes the most obvious personality features of this new leader.

Table 6: Personality Profile of the New Leader

- High energy level

- Healthy family life

- Abundant enthusiasm

- Values self-development

- Communicates effectively and easily

- Intelligent and clear-reasoning

- Uses his or her experience

- Displays a positive and courageous attitude

- Various and simultaneous activities in life

- Seeks out change and is able to take advantage of it

- Tranquil and committed to happiness

- Has self-control (feelings and thoughts)

- Involved in volunteer activities

- Focuses on doing the right thing in the right way

- Actively involved in finding quality of life

Does this remind you of anything? What personality profile have the world's best management and business magazines and most modern institutions been increasingly addressing over the past few years? This profile is more than the result of new management models and academic approaches or technologies (production, planning, and control). It is the product of the gradual evolution of significant portions of humanity from the opportunistic and conformist stages to the self-aware and conscientious stages. This is especially true among the population with greater access to personal transformation methods, such as research and analysis programs, real-time information, and self-transformation and self-improvement through counseling or meditation therapy.

This is a good opportunity to go back to Table 3 in Chapter 3 and review the behavior at each stage of maturity, according to Loevinger's model. Cross-culturization by the Internet; the new digital economy; increased concern about the environment, sustainable development, and individual well-being; and a new global awareness of the needs of the Third World have all helped the collective conscience to mature.

In our terms, the collective psyche has gradually developed something akin to the Seven Cs (so necessary to corporations). This has led many management theorists, opinion makers, and professionals at the decision-making level to become increasingly aware of the need to develop in themselves, their colleagues, and their organizations greater confidence, commitment, cocreation, connection, communication, celebration of successes, and course correction. They also see the need for caring in their relations with others.

This is the new type of professional, and such people should become our new leaders. These men and women are more informed, connected, careful, and committed to the well-being of themselves and those around them. They understand the fundamentals of productivity, profitability, and competition in an environment marked by obvious and growing human diversity. Table 7 shows the differences between the old- and new-style managers.

Table 7: Emergent Leadership

Traditional Leadership	→	Emergent Leadership
Predefined standards	→	Values changes
Shows confidence in the orders given	→	Facilitates and teaches
Supports hierarchy	→	Establishes connections
Individual work	→	Teamwork
Isolation and individualism	→	Participation and team spirit
Knows all the answers	→	Formulates questions or doubts
Limits and defines	→	Helps qualify
Gives orders	→	Sets the example
Transmits orders	→	Empowers

Traditional Leadership	→	Emergent Leadership
Imposes discipline	→	Values creativity
Acts hierarchically	→	Operates in team or network
Military archetype	→	Educator archetype
Keeps people "walking on eggshells"	→	Stimulates with rewards
Rigid	→	Flexible
From above	→	From within
Mechanistic	→	Holistic
Impersonal and objective	→	Personal and subjective
Compartmental	→	Systemic

Over the last few decades, we have experienced the start of a macrocultural transition. We see old-style management techniques coexisting with the new, as flexible organic values gradually replace rigid hierarchicalism. This development causes everyone to feel the creative tension of being anchored in the old reality while creating and living a new one.

At times such as these, our organizations need leaders who are well-prepared for the huge challenge of guiding the transformations that are so important to the survival of their companies. We believe that the leaders of such a demanding transition must have four fundamental characteristics:

1. *Confidence* in the organization as it goes through the transformation, not only to survive but also to succeed, allowing people to mature and advance. Current behavior is merely an expression of a temporary stage on the path toward maturity.

2. *Courage* to challenge the fundamental practices and beliefs upheld by our organizations and society. They must clearly understand that our old behaviors and belief structures are obsolete, although the major part of our societies continues to accept them (especially the hierarchical values system).

3. *Determination* to do their best, insisting on achieving success for themselves, their organizations, and the community to which they belong. As I often say to my son, "If you can only be a C student, then that's the best you can do. However, if you can be an A student and have only gotten Cs, then you are not determined to be the best that you can be."

4. *Willingness* to spend many years of hard work and discipline transforming a rigid hierarchical company into an organic company. This will require persistence, dedication, and discipline. No external consultant or advisor can do this instead of the leader. Consultants should only enrich and facilitate the process.

We must aim for a desired future in which the organization is not following a single leader, whether a charismatic president or a high-powered CEO. Strategic leadership must come from the organizational vision, carried out by leaders at every level of the organization. This is why, when facilitating transformation projects, we take organizations through leadership training. We do this to give leaders at every level the ability to guide the company toward a future that, although still a dream, is one in which everyone will play an important part.

Fundamental Beliefs for Good Leadership

In the 1990s, we conducted a leadership development program for a large industrial group in Brazil. On the first page of the training manual for the program, we called the participants' attention to the following:

> Most Western corporations have lost their sense of Vision and Purpose. If they have a Purpose, they base it on unclear values. Talking to directors and managers, they seem to be concerned only with next quarter's profits or with losing control to an aggressive stockholder. The stakeholders abandon their commitment to the organization that increasingly focuses on mediocrity. Even companies and management theories that praise excellence are in fact praising "excellent mediocrity." How can there be excellence without a purpose, focus, or intense commitment?
>
> The rapid changes brought about by technological innovation that will intensify in the years to come will make our current ways of dealing with reality obsolete. The trends we are seeing lead us to conclude that traditional management methods no longer work. Only by expanding our ways of thinking and creating our Vision of the future will we develop in the

present the foundations for a better future. This is the invitation that we are giving you: let us architect this future together and assure the long-term survival of our companies, to the benefit of all of us as conscious, self-determined beings.

This type of program involves sessions and meetings over a year or more. The sessions give the managers the opportunity to analyze thoroughly and discuss in depth the delicate adjustments that will give the organization the ability to survive the extraordinary changes that are occurring in society and in the business environment. I have decided, therefore, to include in this book several theories and practical exercises that my colleagues and I have adapted for personal sensitization and maturity. They will give you a preliminary evaluation of how much you and your organization need to change to manage the business environment with this new type of leader.

Only Metanoic Organizations Will Survive

To appreciate the survivability of a "metanoic organization," you must understand its characteristics (Senge, 1990), that is, one in which individuals and organizations can create their future and control their destiny. *Metanoic*, from the Greek word *metanoia*, means a fundamental shift of mind. A metanoic organization:

Has an intense sense of purpose

- Knows and cares about its identity and values;

- Understands and admits its purpose;

- Recognizes that its purpose must be aligned with the main issues in societies worldwide;

- Aligns everything it does with its purpose;

- Directs all stakeholders toward achieving the purpose.

Is focused on performance

- Works as a systemic lively unit;

- Specifies and defends its identity and values;

- Values synergy, thus achieving results that go beyond individual efforts;

- Makes individuals focus on themselves and every task to be performed, allowing their own purposes and values to be congruent with the company;

- Aligns all efforts, helping individuals to develop a common sense of purpose, with reaffirmed loyalty to a shared corporate vision.

Values talents and competence

- Captures and strengthens individuals' highest values;

- Positively values creative restlessness;

- Promotes a balanced sense of reasoning and intuition;

- Organizes and guides personal talents toward the purpose, according to the corporate vision;

- Values individual talents and skills, as well as personal management abilities.

Has structural integrity

- Allows all individuals to convert their personal skills into positive results for themselves and the company;

- Supports intensive internal communication, reward systems, guidance support, personnel recruiting, and selection, all according to the company's purpose and vision

- Supports clear designation of authority and responsibility;

- Encourages open sharing of information and management processes.

In a metanoic organization, a leader clearly understands the characteristics of a breakpoint, and that at this particular moment he or she can no longer manage from the perspective of his or her beliefs and experiences.

Most people do not clearly see the need for radical change when they are at a breakpoint. Instead, they are inclined to reinforce and protect the past, intensifying the conflict between the old rules and the new.

Figure 8 in Chapter 5 illustrated the life cycle of companies based on George Land's model. From this, you can see why the re-creation phase in the S-curve is where the tension toward evolution is greatest, as shown in Figure 15. The entire organization looks inward, recognizing, and reaffirming its identity, values, and purpose and then strives for a desired future declared in a corporate vision. The organization must leave behind everything that is no longer useful and develop new skills or expertise while preparing all company members for a new way of life. This invariably leads to basic changes in their values and practices (for managing people, processes, and products), eventually affecting the maturity of all stakeholders.

Often, this reassessment happens as the company is going through a difficult phase. Other times, it is part of a program, such as when the organization decides to regenerate itself, targeting a better, sustainable future.

Whatever the case, this process produces tension. Rather than suggesting a problem, it signals a transition, as the company abandons the old and adopts the new.

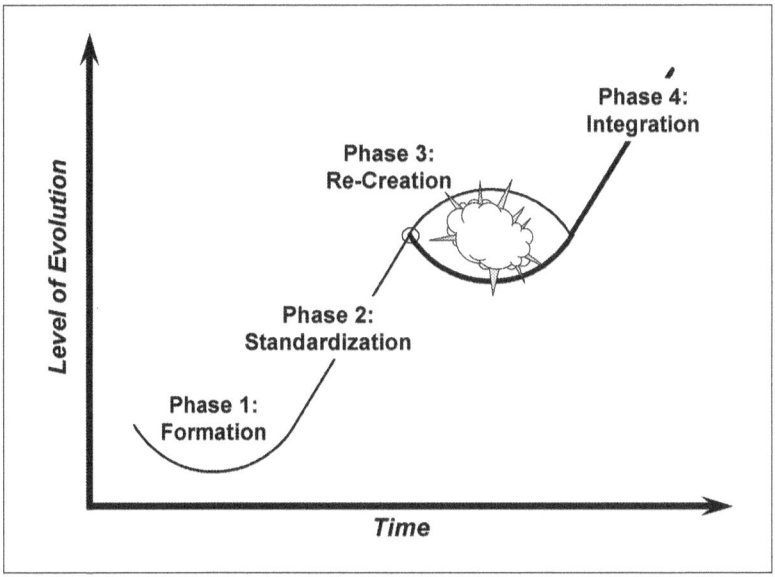

Figure 15: Productive tension at the moment of transition.

At the breakpoint, all the rules of the game drastically and unexpectedly change. The future is not predictable by merely analyzing the past. The behavior of the system also changes in radical terms and new rules violate the principles of the old system. At this point, energies are intense, even though they do not appear to be. If you examine the moment of renewal that marks the point of transition, you can see why the company needs well-prepared

leaders more than ever. They must keep the team and the internal stakeholders united, motivated, and on course towards achieving the collective organizational vision.

Figure 16 shows what happens as the company moves along curve *A*
through the point of inflection. Vectors *a'* and *b'* are both working on the
organization. The need to change applies pulls against all existing processes
and puts stress on the organization as it tries to preserve its past. At this point,
one force dominates and the other fails. The organization either dies (or simply vegetates), or it advances toward better internal integration and congru-
ence with its environment (curve *B*).

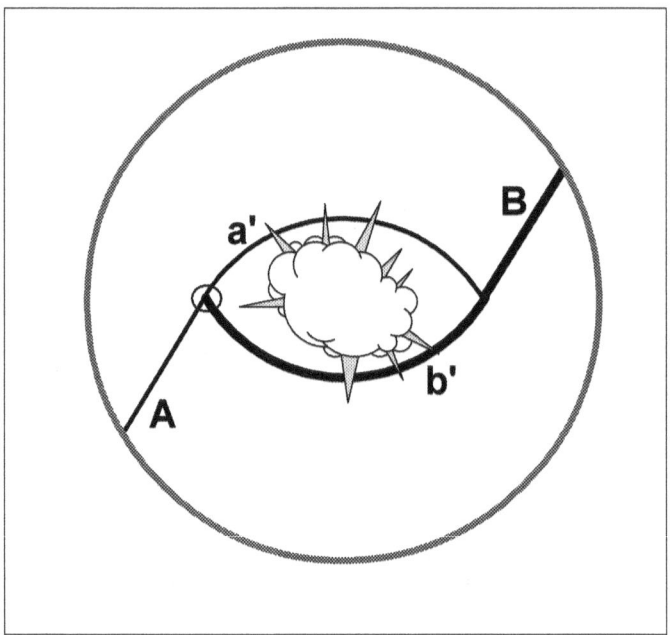

Figure 16: The transition point.

During a successful transition, vector *a'* gradually loses force as vector *b'*
gains strength. This forces the organization to live for a time with two different realities: the old, stable and resistant to change thanks to culture suck; and
the new, in a phase of vigorous renewal, energized by the future pull.

This is a delicate moment, as I said in Chapter 5. This transition point may
be threatening if the organization does not have leaders prepared to support

the process or if the company has no firm commitment to the transformation. Commitment must come from the highest level, including the company's board of directors, the executive management, and controlling shareholders. As we have seen, most individuals in organizations are opportunistic and conformist, with some impulsive individuals, and these maturity levels will naturally fight change.

Everyone is subject to various forms of pressure at the breakpoint, and each responds according to his or her stage of development. Accustomed to being creatures of fate, the impulsive react with fear and aggression, spreading poison and anguish at every turn. The opportunistic place themselves wisely in the hope of new opportunities for personal advancement, behaving more or less cynically. The conformists reaffirm obedience to their comfortable routines, waiting passively for new orders from their superiors. Meanwhile, the self-aware, conscientious, and autonomous, more advanced toward being creators, feel a fresh breeze of change in the organization. They carefully watch what is happening. They are comfortable with change and contradictions. They may even react to it with childlike joy and enthusiasm.

Every single one of them is necessary for the transition, including those that will eventually find themselves excluded from the process. This is because an organization is nothing more than a group of individuals united by common purposes and values; the organization's maturity is the result of the productive interaction between individuals at different levels of maturity.

The enterprise has committed to developing all of its internal stakeholders, as it stated in its identity, values, and purpose. It needs good leaders to manage this diverse collection of personalities, abilities, and needs to achieve more productivity, profitability, and competitiveness. Otherwise, they will lose their talent and become mediocre, as people abandon the company for their own various reasons. The impulsive individuals will search for a better guarantee of having their basic needs satisfied. The opportunistic individuals will shop for what seems the best opportunity for not taking risks. The conformists will target an organization that better fits their personality. The self-aware, conscientious, autonomous, and certainly the integrated will search for better personal growth opportunities, a healthier lifestyle, and a heightened sense of self-improvement.

Evaluating Management Systems

From this point forward, we provide tools to help you make a first (and superficial) diagnosis of the state of the organization for which you work, or for which you are a stakeholder.

Table 8 shows a tool developed by Gustavo Boog, an associate in Corporate Transitions. You can use it to discover the prevailing state of the leadership throughout the organization. Stakeholders rate each characteristic of the company's leadership, on a scale from 1 to 10.

Centered on keeping a balance between achieving business results. Motivating a stimulating environment that is innovative and flexible. Always adding value.	01 02 03 04 05 06 07 08 09 10	Centered on achieving business results even in detriment of people and innovation, excessively focused on activities without added value.
Attitudes and example stimulates accomplishment of the future outcomes.	01 02 03 04 05 06 07 08 09 10	Is neutral or negative about the future and its outcomes
Flexible leadership style, promoting developing his or her subordinates' maturity.	01 02 03 04 05 06 07 08 09 10	Excessively focused on a single leadership style, failing to develop the maturity of his or her subordinates.
Stimulates teamwork spirit and assumes functional responsibilities, managing the process with vision.	01 02 03 04 05 06 07 08 09 10	Focuses individual performance results, without fully exercising his or her functional responsibilities, lacking integral management and vision of the process.
Motivates personnel by publicly recognizing individual contributions.	01 02 03 04 05 06 07 08 09 10	Does not recognize individual contributions, negatively influences personnel.
Is self-motivated and energetic.	01 02 03 04 05 06 07 08 09 10	Shows dislike for his or her functional role.

Keeps the team apprised of relevant information (is open).	01 02 03 04 05 06 07 08 09 10	Totally or partially conceals information and task skills.
Focused on external and internal customers.	01 02 03 04 05 06 07 08 09 10	Focused on production and control.
Keeps a balance between short-term and long-term actions.	01 02 03 04 05 06 07 08 09 10	Focused on short-term immediate results.
Values humanist capacity and ability.	01 02 03 04 05 06 07 08 09 10	Has an excessively technical and specialist vision.
Knows how to act strategically.	01 02 03 04 05 06 07 08 09 10	Performance is limited to tactics (task-oriented).
Actively promotes a better quality of life for himself, the team and the community.	01 02 03 04 05 06 07 08 09 10	Is not concerned with his or her own quality of life, neither that of his or her team or community.
Cooperatively promotes trusting partnerships.	01 02 03 04 05 06 07 08 09 10	Stimulates individualism, manipulates power, misuses control and protects his or her favorites.
Believes in people's innate potential, creating proper conditions for their development.	01 02 03 04 05 06 07 08 09 10	Treats his or her team as if they should simply obey orders while he does all the thinking.
Delegates and negotiates responsibilities, assuring decision-taking autonomy and accountability	01 02 03 04 05 06 07 08 09 10	Imposes responsibility without delegating authority, see-sawing between control and abdication.
Is efficient in managing people.	01 02 03 04 05 06 07 08 09 10	Believes that managing people is up to the human resources department.
Proactively stimulates creativity and positive questioning of the status quo.	01 02 03 04 05 06 07 08 09 10	Stimulates conformance and obedience to the status quo, being strongly reactive.

Admires diversity of opinions and performance.	01 02 03 04 05 06 07 08 09 10	Always searching conforming opinions and performance.
Is always open to reexamining products, processes and performance.	01 02 03 04 05 06 07 08 09 10	Says that "a team that is winning is best left as it is," thus avoiding process and product reviews.
Has a sense of balance between logic and intuition.	01 02 03 04 05 06 07 08 09 10	Focuses only on logic and discourages intuition in day-to-day tasks.
Always acts ethically.	01 02 03 04 05 06 07 08 09 10	Is ethical when convenient.
Promotes pride in the company.	01 02 03 04 05 06 07 08 09 10	Promotes pride in belonging to his or her own area.
Ensures that his or her team of direct subordinates also performs according to this profile.	01 02 03 04 05 06 07 08 09 10	Does not consider himself responsible for the actions or profile of his or her subordinates.

Table 8: How Is Your Company's Leadership?

The results of this survey will help you to see the state of leadership within your organization. Table 9 will help you to analyze how well your company practices each of the Seven Cs. You may want to refer to the description of these fundamental components that you saw in Chapter 3 and analyze your company in light of the concepts explained there.

When using the tool, focus on two fundamental aspects:

1. How well the organization demonstrates the competency and how well you demonstrate it in your personal life;

2. The level of implementation or development of the internal programs and processes that ensure continuous self-renewal.

You may make some errors in your evaluation. This is normal, because of the strong feelings caused by daily life within the company, or given the limited picture that you have of processes and people within a system of hierarchical values. This is why specialists who are unbiased and trained to perform the study and analyze the results should perform a work of this nature. Do not be afraid, however, to do your own test as an initial evaluation.

Table 9: The Level of Development of the Seven Cs

Component	Manifestations	Processes/Systems
Confidence	• People are honest and open in every interpersonal transaction • Is grapevine communication prevalent? • Do people feel prepared with adequate knowledge, skills, and information for their tasks? • Do people affirm that their colleagues know the business?	• How is information gathered, and how is it disseminated? • Is the training and development system adequate? • Is training and development related to the skills and knowledge necessary for the tasks in pursuit of the vision? • Is there a connection between the company's vision and its training and development system?
Commitment	• Do people talk about their work with great enthusiasm? • Is there a strong sense of pride in working for the organization? • Can people clearly express the organization's identity, values, and purpose? • Do people feel the organization's actions are coherent with its purpose? • Does the company effectively live the affirmed values?	• Does the organization have a written statement of its values and purpose? • Have the stakeholders translated the values and purpose into effective attitudes toward the customer? • Does the company have a customer satisfaction feedback system? • Does the company have a system for rewarding exceptional performance and correcting off-course actions when necessary?

Component	Manifestations	Processes/Systems
Cocreation	• Does the company have a written vision statement? • Can internal stakeholders clearly summarize the company's vision of its future? • Do internal stakeholders identify a formal speech associated with the course desired by everyone? • Who is the leader, the corporate vision or the organization's top management?	• Has the vision been translated in to consistent goals, at least in relation to customers, production, people, and finances? • Are internal processes and systems prioritized according to the vision? • Are consensus priorities aligned with the current performance of each vision element?
Connection	• Do people associate their daily tasks with achieving the vision? • Can people describe how the success of their activities determines the vision's fulfillment? • Was enough time and space set aside to manage the transition?	• Is there a transition management system? • Have tasks been precisely defined in terms of what they are and are not? • Are there clear reasons for working in teams rather than as individuals to fulfill the transformation? • Do the teams and individuals have enough authority to perform their tasks?

Component	Manifestations	Processes/Systems
Communication	• People feel they are getting enough feedback about their performance? • Do people get the right information they need to perform their tasks? • Are individuals or teams aware of the tasks of other individuals and teams? • Is there an open communication atmosphere? • Are people overburdened with excess information?	• Is there a manual or digital system that allows coordinating and spreading information quickly? • Is there a well-structured workflow and information flow? • Has the organization clearly established who must get what information and when or why they receive it?
Celebration (and Course Correction)	• Is there a climate of celebration when milestones are achieved? • Do people feel comfortable getting feedback, even when things are not going well?	• Have strategic milestones been established for each task? • Are there clear performance indicators to evaluate the fulfillment of each task? • Is there a system to detect exceptional as well as undesirable performance? • If so, is the system manual or digital?

Component	Manifestations	Processes/Systems
Caring and Crossing	• Are suppliers treated as partners or opponents? • Is the communication between the parts natural or often problematic? • Do the parts respect one another enough, allowing open communication with partners, or is all the information somehow protected?	• Is there a just-in-time process? • Is there a system that allows and supports constant dialog between the parts? • To what extent is information concealed from suppliers and why?

The next step in this preliminary assessment focuses on your personal life within the company.

Self-Evaluating the Company

Internal stakeholders (unless they are at the impulsive or opportunistic stage of maturity) need to recognize their alignment with the identity, values, and purpose of the organization for which he or she works. Otherwise, their sense of goodwill toward their company will gradually decrease, as will their productivity, potentially putting at risk everything that makes the transformation self-sustaining.

As we saw in Chapter 3, an optimal organization will have a vision aligned with a noble purpose. It takes a thousand small steps toward realizing the corporate vision and should have its change process orchestrated, conducted, and carried out by dedicated, creative, caring, and respectful equals. Everything that they do should simultaneously add value to themselves, their families, their company, and their community, while developing their self-esteem and maturity.

So that each internal stakeholder, whether worker or manager, can experience a genuine team spirit in the organization, he or she must see him- or herself as both an individual and as a members of the team. They will be motivated toward improving their own productive and business skills. This will help to transform the company into a learning organization, where they will be able to mature personally in a protected environment, helping them to become more creator than creature, with large benefits to themselves and to the company.

A leadership development program, therefore, also encourages all internal stakeholders to compare their personal values and purposes with those of the company and to understand the degree of compatibility between them. Table 10 is an example of a tool that you can use for this. Remember that these comparisons require maturity and respect for the individual and must be done in a noncompetitive way. Without this step, the Seven Cs will never be completely implanted in the organization.

As you have already seen, the organizational transformation is not a simple task. It must move the organization toward the organic structure that everyone wants, thus affirming the cocreated vision while simultaneously supporting future pull and withstanding culture suck. Can you imagine how difficult this would be if those involved did not share a strong, conscientious commitment? It would be frustrating to try to adopt a new form of management over the public opposition of some and the secret sabotage of others, with serious results for everyone.

Table 10: Alignment Between the Organizational and
Individual Purpose and Values

1.	Where am I with respect to my values, paradigms, and ego development stage?
2.	Where is my company with respect to its values, paradigms, and ego development stage?
3.	What is my personal purpose?
4.	What is my organization's purpose?
5.	How closely are they aligned?
6.	What needs does my company have for its satisfaction that I want to contribute to and that will add value to me and to my organization?
7.	What exactly must I do to create further alignment and true commitment within my organization?
8.	What can I do to turn my purpose and vision into reality?
9.	What project could I develop in my functional area?

10.   What do I need, to do so?

11.   In what ways does this project add value to the organization, to me, to my family, to the community, and to others?

12.   How will people see this project in one or two years?

13.   How will people see it in terms of an interface with customers, production, people, and finances?

14.   What actions or activities will I undertake to fulfill this project?

15.   How are these actions and activities interrelated?

16.   What resources will I need?

17.   What will be the milestones (performance indicators) for each action or activity?

18.   Who will be responsible for each action or activity?

19.   What information does each require? How can I get it?

20.   What are the possible obstacles outside myself? Within myself?

21.   Where will I find support for my project? Who will give me feedback?

22.   What shall I do to celebrate success? With whom? When?

Firm Commitment to the Future

Only a brave personal evaluation, within the process of organizational transformation, will form the company's members (shareholders and employees) into a team. A team that is confident, committed, cocreative, connected, and communicating, that celebrates successes, corrects its course, and cares, all at the same time. A team that works well with the organization, with clients, with suppliers, and with the community. Without this, no organization will be able to survive in this commerce and business environment.

This team must be integrally aligned with the corporate identity, values, purpose, and vision, structured to behave as a healthy organism. It must be able to arrange and—establish its multiple specializations and needs harmoniously at each instant. It must be aimed toward this objective: to produce better with more well-being, less expense, and better survivability. It must be composed of creators in distinct levels of preparation and directed by true leaders, forged or born in the transformation process itself.

The leaders must be the guardians of the future as depicted in the corporate vision. They must communicate it in a clear and precise form, in a caring and respectful way.

Above all, a leadership development program also should help the participants to develop the abilities listed in Table 11.

Table 11: Good Communication, the Key to Success

- Have a clear picture of what you want others to understand;

- Think about the best attitude to present the topic or information;

- Think about what you feel toward the people with whom you are about to communicate;

- Consider your own communication abilities;

- Consider the communication abilities of your audience;

- Adapt the message to your audience's situation and abilities;

- Initiate communicating in as simple a form as possible;

- Develop one idea at a time, one step at a time;

- Compare and contrast ideas, associating the unknown and the known;

- Decide precisely which ideas need special emphasis;

- Build mechanisms to obtain real-time and dynamic feedback;

- Allow room for the flow of information.

Leaders Tell Us Who We Are—Leaders connect with the reasons behind the company's formation, integrating the past with the future, communicating a sense of organizational identity and purpose.

Leaders Tell Us Where We Are Going—Leaders communicate the vision of a desired future and why the company would want such a future. Thus, they communicate the goals, and how achieving these goals is useful to the organization, its customers and stakeholders

Leaders Tell Us How Things Will Feel—Leaders clearly show how important and exciting working toward the vision will be, so that all stakeholders see the relevance of their work to their own lives.

Leaders Tell Us What We Can Do—Leaders transmit a sense of value to each person and reaffirm the importance of individual efforts, so that everyone in the organization (including shareholders and employees) clearly understands their role in the overall mission.

Leaders Tell Us How We Will Do What Has to Be Done—Leaders communicate the achievement strategy clearly, suggesting values and priorities, guiding people, and passing on a sense of urgency in what they do together, as a unified and cooperative force aimed toward the vision.

Leaders Communicate How Much They Believe in Us—Leaders reaffirm their faith and confidence in their colleagues and subordinates, in a way that everyone feels capable and confident toward pursuing the vision from within its identity, values, and purpose.

Thus, leaders and the led, managers or workers, will move with certainty toward a lively, agile, productive, profitable, and self-sustaining organization. It will be a renewed organization with eyes focused on its future, based on its history, identity, values, and purpose, through the continuous work of its shareholders and employees. It will be an organization that is committed to lasting development and more able to satisfy the needs of its customers through rewarding partnerships with suppliers—one that is prepared to attend to the needs of all its stakeholders and the community in which it exists. It will be able to sail the tsunamis of change that are sure to confront it.

Chapter 10

The Moral Organization

In this book, I have been talking about Organizational Architecture. I have been inviting you and your company to engage in reinventing yourselves and thus our world. I have proposed a gentle renewal of the organizational structure, transforming your values system from hierarchical to organic. I have shown that this method improves productivity, profitability, and long-term survivability. I have proposed a method that will allow your internal stakeholders to rise to higher managerial and personal maturity. It is a method that can lead your organization and its stakeholders towards becoming self-aware, conscientious, and autonomous creators of an exciting, successful future.

Leaders Have Only One Choice

In today's business climate, no other alternative exists than to architect your organization with the necessary structures and processes that will allow them to sail any tsunamis they may face. Organizations urgently need the tools, skills, processes, and knowledge that will allow them to renew themselves continuously in a positive and self-sustaining way. Through the process of architecting, organizations can overcome the challenge of simultaneously increasing productivity, profitability, and competitiveness while satisfying customer needs and thus winning their loyalty. It is important to improve the quality of life for your stakeholders, making work in your company a source of motivation, accomplishment, and happiness, with respect for society and the natural environment.

In Chapter 1, I discussed the studies carried out by former Harvard professor Lawrence Kohlberg, that clearly showed that people only develop ethically and morally through psychoemotional evolution. According to his "moral maturity" model, the ethical behavior of individuals changes as they progress through the successive stages of maturity. Although not measured, we saw a similarity to the models proposed by Abraham Maslow, Erik Erickson, and Jane Loevinger.

We saw that the *preconventional* morality level clearly corresponds to Loevinger's impulsive and opportunistic stages, whereas Kohlberg's *conventional* morality level characterizes Loevinger/Pinedo-Lasker's conformist, self-aware, and conscientious stages. Loevinger's, autonomous and integrated stages correlated with Kohlberg has the most advanced *postconventional* morality level.

Maturity Is the Key

Our process significantly helps internal stakeholders to mature, and this helps to improve production, management, and business processes. Through active intervention in the corporation's culture, structure, and communication, the organization and its stakeholders act with greater social integrity, relevance, and survivability. Once the organization starts behaving organically, it accepts its moral responsibilities toward the environment, other organizations, and the community in which it exists. This encourages internal and external stakeholders to engage in activities that lessen the potential causes of social tsunamis.

Only by promoting collective maturity and postconventional ethics will we prevent disgraces such as the scandals at Enron, Andersen Accounting, and Tyco. There have been similar instances in the past, at Baring's Bank in England and others. These events had a significant negative impact on national economies and stock markets. Examples that affected whole societies and countries include the riots in Curaçao and the crises in Argentina and Venezuela, where the rigid hierarchical values have caused the government to decline in the first case and a near revolution in the second.

These examples reveal more than individual character flaws or errors in assessment and decision making. They show how leadership that is immature both developmentally and morally can cause large-scale damage. It is worth noting that morality means acting honestly even when such actions are obviously disadvantageous. When morality is lacking, as it is at the lower levels of maturity, bad things happen. The costs incurred in damage control and follow-up—no matter how efficient these activities may be—significantly reduce profitability and create unnecessary stress on organizations.

It is important to begin efforts to help populations to advance their ego stages. This is not just to give companies better business and production capacity and reduce their mass of deadwood, and unproductive internal processes, but to transform society into a more effective and satisfying framework for human life. Above all, we must involve many more people in transforming the inhuman conditions imposed by rigid hierarchical values.

The global marketplace is putting pressure on companies and the capital markets that they support to set up practices that are healthier, more open, more participative, more decentralized, and more ethical. This transformation includes the weakening of the roles of CEOs and other traditional leaders. The unenlightened or immature will surely resist this change. The board of directors must take responsibility for making this happen.

This takes me back thirty years, to when the events in Curaçao revealed that something was fundamentally wrong in the country's social and business structure. We had been managing under the notion that all we had to do is continue to improve, little by little, correcting defects here and there, toward a better world. The riots proved this assumption disastrous, and changed my life forever.

The Principles of Organizational Architecture

Since the Curaçao riots, my cause has been to transform companies' hierarchical business and production structures changing the socioeconomic and cultural matrix that shelters, sustains, and justifies them. In due course, this gave birth to a process that I see as the distillation of my guiding beliefs that became the principles of Organizational Architecture:

- Organizations (and people) are born, mature (or stagnate), age (prematurely or not), and die (although organizations can re-create themselves).

- Few organizations (and few people) manage to reach full maturity or peak performance, whereas some prefer mediocrity, persistently striving for the best mediocrity possible.

- After maturing, organizations (and people) must live independently of their founders' (or parents).

- In the vast history of civilizations, a new form of human existence is emerging, in a metanoic process (to transform beyond, based on something that exists), toward organizations in which work is conscious, gratifying, and fulfilling.

- Also, today's obsolete structures value the obedient follower over the creative rebel, which explains why our cultures are inhabited by creatures rather than creators.

- Therefore, we shall only be set free if we design and set up structures that promote the essential competencies and creator values, allowing everyone to stop acting as creatures. We shall then be endowed with the power to create rules that will guide us in the search of greater well-being and thus a more productive, profitable, and sustainable way of life.

Several important indicators confirm that the rigid hierarchical structures that have conditioned us for centuries are failing:

- Companies whose organizational values are focused on short-term financial profitability are going bankrupt.

- All sectors of the economy are becoming less productive.

- Companies are desperately searching for adding value through mergers and takeovers.

- The needy population is expanding, even in central markets of the world economy.

- There has been an endless exodus of talent to competitors or risky endeavors for which they are unprepared.

- There has been a brutal decrease of commitment to companies (from shareholders, employees, customers, suppliers, and the community).

All these indicators clearly signal the significant need (that has been around since the 1960s) to reinvent how private and public organizations work. They are in danger, even though they do not realize or admit it.

New Business Structures Needed

For this specific reason, we need business structures that work much more effectively than the hierarchical model that currently drives most organizations, in which the opportunistic and conformist stages of maturity prevail. Otherwise, dissatisfaction will continue to grow at all levels will bring about the radical and violent destruction of our present forms of business and society.

Hierarchy was essential to the design of the production line, the nucleus of the Industrial Revolution. However, over time industrial production is becoming less important to the global economy, just as industry gained supremacy over agriculture during the Industrial Revolution.

Before the start of the twentieth century, agriculture made up the major economic segment of the economy. In most of the developed countries today, agriculture represents only a small fraction (~3%) of the Gross Domestic Product (GDP). In the United States, agriculture does not exceed 2 percent of the GDP.

Like agriculture, manufacturing is also on the decline in developed countries. In 1960, for example, manufacturing was central to the economies in all developed countries. By 1999, manufacturing's percentage of the GDP dropped drastically, barely exceeding 15 percent. In 2000, the financial sector easily surpassed manufacturing in contributing to the GDP.

The same is occurring in all developing countries. In São Paulo, Brazil, for example, during the 1980s services created one job for every job in the manufacturing sector. Fifteen years later, services were producing three times the employment opportunities that manufacturing offered.

However, today's economy is service-based. Information technology is the driving force, and modern structures must allow humans to interact in distinctly different ways. These structures will enable organizations to function effectively and with sustained efficiency while helping people and the organization to mature and take the fundamental steps to advance from creatures to creators. This implies processes that favor and promote corporate democracy and transformation, without which they will not survive in this globalized world.

Survival Requires Fundamental Change

For an organization to survive, it will need to do more than make mere improvements to its production, administration, and human-interaction processes. Survival will require deep cultural and structural transformation. The organization must raise its level of consciousness through the Seven Cs and by helping its internal stakeholders to mature emotionally and managerially.

At the same time, organizations must become actively engaged in the task of helping their societies to mature, collectively replacing the hierarchical structures left behind by the opportunistic- and conformist-stage thinking. In order to address organizations' structure and dynamics of production and management processes, one must address values, relationship dynamics, and stages of ego development. Otherwise, there will be no change in organizational culture, no space for human creativity, no increase in productivity, and no sustained well-being and progress.

It is as simple as that—and as unavoidable.

Unless we change our structural and values system from elitist, hierarchical values systems to organic ones, tsunamis will continue to cause destruction. I saw this happen in Curaçao on May 30, 1969, and, sadly, again on September 11, 2001, in New York City.

I am happy to see morality reawakening in many leaders of our global society. Although this is due in part to the many destructive world events we have witnessed in the last two years, we seem to be at the threshold of a social, political, and economical renaissance. I hope that in this book, organizational leaders will find the necessary ingredients to build the new organic structures needed to sail their organizations through any tsunami they may face.

> It was the best of times, it was the worst of times, it was the age of wisdom, it was the age of foolishness…It was the spring of hope, it was the winter of despair, we had everything before us, we had nothing before us.

These words, written by Charles Dickens in *A Tale of Two Cities* in 1859, describe a period of turmoil in France. The elitist hierarchy was crumbling. Louis XV, Louis XVI, and other leaders at the time chose to ignore the many signs around them of widespread discontent and refused to see that fundamental change was on the way. The result was one of the most violent tsunamis in history: the French Revolution.

Dickens could have written those words to describe the times today. Unlike the French kings, our leaders have the tools and the ability to prepare for the coming tsunami, if they will. Our leaders have a choice:

Ensure profitability, sustainability, and more ethical behavior through Organizational Architecture,

Or

Preserve the elitist, hierarchical systems that we are so used to and produce another revolution!

Chapter 11

The Legacy of the *Tsunami*

Two thousand four was the year of the tsunamis. I published the first edition of this book at the start of the year. Its end was marked by the great tsunami in the Indian Ocean, which proved to be one of the largest and deadliest natural disasters in recent history. It left hundreds of thousands of people dead, and vividly defined the word tsunami in the minds of billions.

As I said in the foreword, my first reaction to this catastrophe was to delay publication of this second edition out of respect for those who perished. I did not want to appear to be trying to profit from others' misfortune. Upon reflection, however, I decided that people's heightened awareness of the dangers of natural tsunamis would make this the ideal moment to do go forward with the second edition. My purpose in publishing this book was to help organizations and societies avoid or even prevent catastrophic business tsunamis; if the generally heightened awareness of natural tsunamis would help to get this important message out, then I should proceed. Perhaps, having recently seen the destructive power of a tsunami in nature and having read this method for avoiding and preventing these catastrophes in the business world, you are now ready to start down the road to a sustainable, resilient, and mature organization, the process that I call Organizational Architecture.

The Virtuality Revolution

Tsunamis of different sizes are washing over the business world all the time these days. Computers and the Internet are relentlessly changing our way of doing business. The result is—and will continue to be—many sudden, drastic shifts in the marketplace and even the collapse of massive industry giants.

Not since the Industrial Revolution have we seen such a radical change in the way that customers perceive quality, service, and value; nor has competition changed so rapidly. Not since the Industrial Revolution has there been such a threat to companies' very survival...nor has there been so much opportunity for those prepared to seize it!

Never before have customers been presented with so much information and so many choices, nor have customers' needs and requirements changed so quickly. Never before have companies' survival depended so completely upon their agility, resilience, and organizational maturity.

Not only are we seeing massive waves of change, but also the waves are coming with increasing frequency. Take the Agricultural Age, for example. It was the result of the Agricultural Revolution and lasted for thousands of years with the marketplace essentially unchanged. Then the Industrial Revolution came along and fundamentally redefined not only the marketplace but also the very definition of capital. Only a hundred and fifty years later, we were in the middle of the next wave, the Electronics Revolution. Two short decades later came the Computer Revolution, followed in very short order by the Information Revolution. Each of these has made and destroyed fortunes and even industries.

As I said earlier in this book, we are at present in the middle of what I call the *Virtuality Revolution*, in which "any time, any place" technology is breaking down physical barriers. I foresee that in short order a new tsunami will shake our world: the *Intelligence Revolution*. It will see artificial intelligence taking care of more and more mundane tasks, freeing human intellect for strategic thinking, problem solving, and relationship building...the most human of tasks.

The tsunamis have washed and will wash away those who cannot or will not adapt. Yesterday's market is not tomorrow's or even today's market. Yesterday's way of doing business will not satisfy the needs of tomorrow's customers. Tsunamis will wash away companies that are prepared *only* for yesterday's marketplace. Companies whose structures and skills are adapted to the violent nature of the new business climate will survive and thrive.

Companies who learn how to sail a tsunami see specific benefits. Most see increased profitability due to improved efficiency and morale as they stop wasting time and money on internal friction and politics. Over time, they see an increase in market share due to their improved ability to seize opportunities and to compete. They notice that stakeholders (customers, suppliers, stockholders, employees, etc.) become more loyal. Their workforce becomes more effective, and an enhanced organizational structure gives the organization the ability to make excellent decisions with dependable regularity. In the long run, most importantly of all, they gain agility and resilience. This gives them the ability not only to survive threats (such as tsunamis), but to take advantage of the opportunities inherent in them.

Do You Have What It Takes to Prosper?

Where are you today? Can your company prosper, even in a tsunami?

Business is a lot like sailing. Like the wind, your customers' needs push you along, or they can push you over. The marketplace, like the ocean, is your medium for success or failure. In a calm ocean, almost any sailboat will get you where you are going. To survive and prosper when beset by tsunamis, however, you will need a new kind of sailboat. Your organizational structure must be agile and resilient, and it must be equipped with special tools, procedures, and equipment to perform in such a hostile environment. You need a crew that is mature, highly trained, strong, and effective, that is able to sail your boat in extreme conditions. You need a clear, step-by-step plan for not merely surviving a tsunami, but thriving in that environment, a plan that is known by every member of the crew and that they have practiced over and over again until it is second nature to them.

You also need a special detection system to avoid dangers. Wild animals proved this on the eve of the Indian Ocean tsunami. While hundreds of thousands of humans sadly perished, wild animals almost completely escaped the devastation. News stories that appeared just after the disaster reported that their highly developed senses allowed them to run for higher ground in time to survive (the newspapers called this a sixth sense).

Take for example this excerpt from an article in New Zealand's National Business on January 6, 2005 entitled, "Asia & Pacific Tsunami: Animals Fled, a Warning Missed":

> [In] Sri Lanka, where tens of thousands lost their lives to the Boxing Day tsunami, animals appear to have fled inland before the waves struck…Giant waves washed floodwaters up to 3 km inland at Yala National Park…Sri Lanka's biggest wildlife reserve and home to hundreds of wild elephants and several leopards…"The strange thing is we haven't recorded any dead animals," [said] HD Ratnayake, deputy director of the national Wildlife Department. "No elephants are dead, not even a dead hare or rabbit." He

added, "I think animals can sense disaster. They have a sixth sense [sic]. They know when things are happening."

In another article on January 5, 2005, in the *Hindustan Times*, Dr. Ranjith Premalal De Silva, an expert in geological information systems, made a similar statement. "Animals in the Yala National Park in south Sri Lanka might have felt tell-tale signs of the tsunami three or four days ahead of the strike on December 26, and that is why there has been no report of animal death from there...Yala is known for its elephants. But not a single elephant was killed! And Yala was one of the worst-hit areas in Sri Lanka."

Although humans apparently lack this ability to detect tsunamis, they can build and install devices that do. For example, both the Japanese and the Hawaiians, who are subject to frequent tsunamis have built systems that do warn people of their approach. The people are also trained in what to do when the alarm sounds. These structures have saved many lives and have the potential for saving millions. Organizations must also put detection systems in place to detect business tsunamis so that they can anticipate them and take advantage of them.

It's undeniably important to know that danger is on the way, but simply knowing is not enough. The real question is, "Can you survive it?"

Is your current sailboat a wallowing, leaky tub on the verge of falling apart or capsizing? Or even merely a good fair-weather boat? No matter how hard you try, you can't make a slow, wallowing tub into the agile, strong, sleek, and resilient vessel that you will need to get you through a tsunami. You need to build a new boat, designed from the keel up to survive tsunamis.

Is your crew unprepared? Are they self-focused, engaging in politics, more concerned with pay and promotion than with getting to port profitably, safely, and on schedule? Do you feel becalmed or adrift, unsure where you are going? Even if *you* know your strategy, does your crew? Is anyone acting on it? To survive a tsunami, a crew must be superbly trained, highly skilled, confident, committed, and mature to successfully sail this new boat through the giant waves.

Will the tsunami find you unaware and unable? Is your sailboat already in trouble? One of the strongest images from the Indian Ocean tsunami showed some boats—poorly constructed or whose crews were caught by surprise—being tumbled like dice or smashed into kindling. Other boats and crews—well-prepared, well-designed, agile, and resilient—turned to and sailed smartly through the giant waves unscathed.

How do you make your organization one of these boats that can sail through tsunamis? Let us briefly review the process that was proposed in previous chapters.

A Review of the Approach

Remember that I suggested that you start with a diagnosis of your organization's current reality. As I said, you must evaluate your existing strategies and current level of situational awareness and define the good features of your current boat that you want to have in the new one. You must inventory and assess your existing tools and equipment, and measure your crew's current skills, knowledge, abilities, attitudes, and overall level of maturity. Knowing what you have is the first step toward knowing what you need.

Next, you need to increase your crew's confidence in the organization and their commitment to it by getting them involved in its strategic planning. This helps give them the will to embark on the architecture process as well as the tenacity to stick with it even in rough waters. You do this by clarifying why the organization exists (its purpose), its guiding beliefs (values), and by cocreating with your crew a preliminary idea of what the organization wants to look like in the future (vision).

Next, you must help your crew learn how to scan the business environment, looking for trends, and *opporthreats* in those trends. Based on the environmental scans, the entire crew cocreates a detailed strategic vision. This is the design for your tsunami-proof sailboat. The strategic vision leads to a detailed strategic map, the plotted course to where you are going.

You will need to cocreate with your crew a master implementation plan to construct and launch your new, tsunami-proof sailboat, and to train the crew to sail it. This plan is a breakdown of the vision into discrete steps, organized to get you there efficiently.

The next step, if you recall, will be to formally launch the strategic plan by installing and initiating the transition management board (TMB). They are the steering committee whose responsibility is for bringing the vision into being. The TMB will select the first mission teams who, under their guidance, will construct the new sailboat (the operational model). The very process of working together to build the new boat will fully align your new processes, your crew (people), and your specialized equipment (technology) with the strategy (information).

As the new boat nears completion, you will equip it with the right tools and technology. Your crew will train, practice, and rehearse operating your new boat in a tsunami-rich environment *before* you leave port. You will refine your charts and planning to meet any changes to the environment.

When all is ready, your new boat will set sail. Your technology will help you effectively monitor your course and position. You will have efficient communications throughout the boat, and your confident crew will work as a harmonious whole. Your ability to measure where you are versus where you had planned to be will allow you to celebrate success and to correct inappropriate behavior. Over time, you will adjust your strategy, plans, and metrics to changes in conditions.

You will find that the boundaries between internal and external stakeholders (suppliers and customers) begin to blur. You will create win-win strategic partnerships. External stakeholders will become more involved with the organization's strategic planning process. Barriers to efficient and effective communication among all internal and external stakeholders will crumble.

It is at this point that you realize that you and your crew will have learned the process. You have excellent technology for communication, process, and project management as well as for control. You and your crew can renew and revise your company at any time in the future. Your environmental scans warn you in plenty of time to adapt to change. When the next tsunami comes along, your organization will be ready.

Conclusion

In this book, I have been trying to show you that our world has been going through many social and business tsunamis. September 11, for example, changed our world forever. Chavez's revolution in Venezuela is still producing ripples on our world's economic oceans. Iran, China, and North Korea are tsunamis waiting to happen. In the business world I have seen tsunamis like the dot-com collapse, the Wall Street crash, and the destruction of Enron, WorldCom, Parmalat, and Ahold. I hope I have given you many ideas and tools that will help your organization become an agile and resilient sailboat that can truly sail through the many tsunamis that you will face in the near future. I hope that I have given you the ability to be proactive, to detect the tsunami, and to avoid its destruction through preparation.

I have tried to show you that a shared organizational purpose and a clearly defined set of values provide are the keel of the tsunami-proof sailboat. They are the basis on which everything else rests.

I hope that you can understand the power of commitment. It helps your crew turn the purpose and values into daily behaviors with your clients and the marketplace. I hope that you have been able to see the power of a strong vision. I hope that you see the value of a clear, cocreated and universally shared strategy, with which the whole organization is aligned and toward which every member of the organization is working. I hope that with this shared direction, you are able to build the right structures and processes; that these will give you the agility, resilience, and strength to go through the many tsunamis you will be confronting.

I hope that you have learned about the importance of effective, real-time communication. I hope that that you have found the tools to put technologies and practice in place that give your organization the ability to predict and survive any tsunami.

I hope that you have seen the importance of celebrating successes and of creating an organization that learns from every one of its experiences in the marketplace and therefore becomes more resilient with each successive generation.

I hope that you have learned to correct off-course behavior in such a way that adversity—rather than leaving scars on your organization—leads to deeper caring among your crew. This in turn leads to more caring relations between all colleagues, suppliers, and clients—even the whole marketplace or society. The loyalty of your stakeholders for your organization will ensure its surviving any storm, and will add value to all who interact with it.

The great tsunami in the Indian Ocean showed on one hand how unprepared we are for unexpected disasters, and on the other how the global community can come together to repair, restore, and improve in their aftermath. We can indeed create better, more resilient organizations and better communities. May reading these pages give you the ideas, tools, and above all the desire to build a new boat in which you can sail tsunamis.

Selected Bibliography

Adams, John. *Transforming Leadership.* Alexandria, VA: Miles River Press, 1986.

Adizes, Ichak. *How to Solve the Mismanagement Crisis.* Santa Monica, CA: Adizes Institute Books, 1985.

Adizes, Ichak. *Corporate Lifecycles: How and Why Corporations Grow and Die and What to Do about It.* Englewood Cliffs: Prentice Hall, 1988.

Adler, Nancy J. "Cross-cultural Management Research: the Ostrich and the Trend." *Academy of Management Review* 8(2):226–232.

Adler, Nancy J. *International Dimensions of Organizational Behavior.* Boston: South-Western, 1997.

Adorno, T. W. and others. *The Authoritarian Personality.* New York: Harper & Row, 1950.

Allport, G. W. *Personality: A Psychological Interpretation.* New York: Holt, Rinehart and Winston, 1937.

Allport, G. W. The Ego in Contemporary Psychology. *Psychological Review* 50(1943): 451–478.

Alper, T. G. Achievement Motivation in College Women: A Now You-See-It-Now-You-Don't Phenomenon. *Am. Psychologist* 29(1974):194–203.

Anderson, S. and others. *Encyclopedia of Educational Evaluation.* San Francisco: Jossey Bass, 1975.

Anderson, W., and R. Dynes. *Social Movements, Violence and Change: The May Movement in Curaçao.* Columbus, OH: Ohio State University Press, 1975.

Angyal, A. *Neurosis and Treatment: A Holistic Theory.* New York: Wiley, 1965.

Atkinson, J. W., and D. C. McClelland. "The Projective Expression of Needs. II. The Effect of Different Intensities of the Hunger Drive on Thematic Apperception." *Journal of Experimental Psychology* 38(3):643–658.

Atkinson, J. W. The Achievement Motive and Recall of Interrupted and Completed Tasks. *Journal of Experimental Psychology* 46(1953):381–390.

Atkinson, J. W., and A. C. Raphelson. Individual Differences in Motivation and Behavior in Particular Situations. *Journal of Personality* 24(1956):349–363.

Atkinson, J. W., and Reitman, W. R. Performance as a Function of Motive Strength and Expectancy of Goal-attainment. *Journal of Abnormal Social Psychology* 53(1956):361–366.

Atkinson, J. W., ed. *Motives in Fantasy, Action and Society.* New York: Van Nostrand, 1958.

Atkinson, J. W., and G. H. Litwin. Achievement Motive and Test Anxiety Conceived as Motive to Approach Success and Motive to Avoid Failure. *Journal of Abnormal Social Psychology* 60(1960):52–63.

Atkinson, J. W., and others. The Achievement Motive, Goal Setting, and Probability Preferences. *Journal of Abnormal Social Psychology* 60(1960):27–36.

Atkinson, J. W., and W. T. Feather. *A Theory of Achievement Motivation.* New York: John Wiley and Sons, 1966.

Atkinson, J. W., and J. E. Raynor. *Motivation and Achievement.* New York: Winston, Wiley, 1974.

Ausubel, D. P. *Ego Development and the Personality Disorders.* New York: Grune and Stratton, 1952.

Baldwin, J. M. *Thought and Things: A Study of the Development and Meaning of Thought, or Genetic Logic.* New York: Arno Press, 1975.

Bales, R. F. *Personality and Interpersonal Behavior.* New York: Holt, Rinehart & Winston, 1970.

Bandura, A., and R. Walters. *Adolescent Aggression.* New York: Roland Press, 1963.

Banfield, E. *The Moral Basis of a Backward Society.* Glencoe, IL: Free Press, 1958.

Bendig, A. W. Comparative Validity of Objective and Projective Measures of Need Achievement in Predicting Students' Achievement in Introductory Psychology. *Journal of General Psychology* 60(1959):237–243.

Bennis, Warren, and Burt Nanus. *Leaders, Strategies for Taking Charge.* New York: Harper Business Press, 1985.

Berlew, D., and W. LeClere. Social Intervention in Curaçao: A Case Study. *Journal of Applied Behavioral Science* 10(1):29–52.

Berne, E. *Games People Play: The Psychology of Human Relationships.* New York: Grove Press, 1964.

Bernstein, B. *Class, Codes and Control (Vol. I).* London: Routledge & Kegan Paul, 1971.

Bethune, Gordon. *From Worst to First.* New York: John Wiley & Sons, 1998.

Boog, Gustavo. *O Desafio da Competência.* São Paulo: Best-Seller, 1991.

Child, John. Theorizing About Organizations Cross-nationally. *Advances in Comparative International Management* 13(1999):27–75.

Crozier, Michael. *The Bureaucratic Phenomenon.* Chicago: University Press, 1964.

Dannemiller Tyson Associates. *Whole-scale Change: Unleashing the Magic in Organizations.* San Francisco: Berret Koehler Publications, 2000.

de Mooij, M. Masculinity/Femininity and Consumer Behavior. In *Masculinity and Femininity: The Taboo Dimension of National Cultures,* ed. G. H. Hofstede. Thousand Oaks, CA: Sage, 1998.

de Tocqueville, Alexis. *Democracy in America.* New York: New American Library, 1956.

Denison, Daniel. R., and A. K. Mishra. Toward a Theory or Organizational Culture and Effectiveness. *Organization Science: A journal of the Institute of Management Sciences* 6(2):204–223.

Durkheim, Emile. *Le Suicide: Etude de Sociologie.* Paris: Press Universitaires de France, 1930.

Earley, P. C. Self or group? Cultural Effects of Training on Self-Efficacy and Performance. *Administrative Science Quarterly* 39(1):89–117.

England, George W. *The Manager and His Values: an International Perspective from the U.S., Japan, Korea, India and Australia.* Cambridge: Ballinger, 1975.

Esteves, Sergio A.P. *O Dragão e a Borboleta.* São Paulo: Axis Mundi, 2000.

Ferrell, O. C., and Steven J. Skinner. Ethical Behavior and Bureaucratic Structure in Marketing Research Organizations. *Journal of Marketing Research* 25(1):103–109.

Frankl, Viktor E. *Man's Search for Meaning.* New York: Washington Square Press, Simon and Schuster, 1963.

Haire, Mason, and others. *Managerial Thinking: an International Study.* New York: John Wiley, 1966.

Hall, M. R. *Understanding Cultural Differences.* Yarmouth, ME: Intercultural Press, 1990.

Hammer, Michael, and James Champy. *Reengineering the Corporation.* New York: Harper Business Press, 1993.

Harrison, R. Understanding Your Organization's Character. *Harvard Business Review,* May-June 1972: 119–128.

Hersey, P., and K. H. Blanchard. *Management of Organizational Behavior: Utilizing Human Resources, 2nd ed.* Englewood Cliffs: Prentice-Hall, 1972.

Hersey, P., and K. H. Blanchard. Leader Effectiveness and Adaptability Description (LEAD). In *The 1976 Annual Handbook for Group Facilitators,* eds. J. W. Pfeiffer & J. E. Jones, La Jolla: University Associates, 1976.

Hofstede, G. H., and others. *Masculinity and Femininity: the Taboo Dimension of National Cultures.* Thousand Oaks, CA: Sage, 1998.

Hofstede, G. H., and others. What Goals do Business Leaders Pursue? A Study in Fifteen Countries. *Journal of International Business Studies* 33(4):785–803.

Knapp, R. H. N Achievement and Aesthetic Preference. In *Motives in Fantasy, Action, and Society,* ed. J. W. Atkinson, 367–372. Princeton: Van Nostrand, 1958.

Knapp, R. H., and J. T. Garbutt. Time Imagery and the Achievement Motive. *Journal of Personality* 26(1958):426–434.

Kohlberg, L. The Development of Children's Orientations Towards a Moral Order. I: Sequence in the Development of Moral Thought. *Vita Humana* 6(1963):11–33.

Kohlberg, L. Development of Moral Character and Moral Ideology. In *Review of Child Development Research. Vol. 1,* eds. M. Hoffman and L. Hoffman, 232–256. New York: Russell Sage, 1964.

Kohlberg, L. From Is to Ought: How to Commit the Naturalistic Fallacy and Get Away with It in the Study of Moral Development. In *Psychology and Genetic Epistemology,* ed. T. Mischel, 151–213. New York: Academic Press, 1971.

Kohlberg, L., and R. Mayer. Development as the Aim of Education. *Harvard Educational Review* 42(4):449–496.

Kohlberg, L. Continuities in Childhood and Adult Moral Development Revisited. In *Life-span Developmental Psychology: Personality and Socialization*, eds. P. Baltes and K. Schaie, 180–207. New York: Academic Press, 1973.

Kohlberg, L., and R. Selman, R. The Relationship Between Perspective-Taking Stage and Moral Judgment. Mimeographed paper. Cambridge: Laboratory of Human Development, Harvard Graduate School of Education; 1973.

Kohlberg, L. *The Meaning and Measurement of Moral Development.* Massachusetts: Clark University Press, 1981.

Kohn, M. *Class and Conformity.* Homewood, IL: Dorsey Press, 1969.

Kolb. D. A., and R. Fry. Toward an Applied Theory of Experiential Learning. In *Theories of Group Process*, ed. C. Cooper. London: John Wiley, 1975.

Kolb, D. A. *The Learning Style Inventory: Technical Manual.* Boston: McBer, 1976.

Kuhn, T. S. *The Structure of Scientific Revolutions, 2nd ed.* Chicago: University of Chicago Press, 1970.

Kusatsu, O. Ego Development and Socio-Cultural Process in Japan (I). *Journal of Economics* 3(1)(1977).

Kusatsu, O. Ego Development and Socio-Cultural Process in Japan (II). *Journal of Economics* 3(2)(1978).

Lambert, H. V. A Comparison of Jane Loevinger's Theory of Ego Development and Lawrence Kohlberg's Theory of Moral Development. Unpublished Ph.D. diss., University of Chicago, 1972.

Land, George. *Grow or Die, the Unifying Principle of Growth.* New York: John Wiley & Sons, 1986.

Land, George, and Jarman Beth Ainsworth. *Breakpoint and Beyond.* New York: Harper Business, 1992.

Lasker, H. M. Factors Affecting Responses to Achievement Motivation Training in India. Unpublished A. B. thesis. Department of Social Relations, Harvard College, 1966.

Lasker, H. M., and C. DeWindt. Ego Development Scoring Manual: Male Responses in a Developing Nation. Mimeographed paper. Willemstad, Curaçao: Fundashon Humanas, 1972.

Lasker, H. M. Some Notes on the Delta/3 Stage. Paper presented to Conference on Ego Development. Washington University, 1973.

Lasker, H. M., and others. Stage-specific Reactions to Ego Development Training. Mimeographed paper. Willemstad, Curaçao: Fundashon Humanas, 1974.

Lasker, H. M. Interim Summative Evaluation Report: Shell O.D. Program. Mimeographed paper. Willemstad, Curaçao: Fundashon Humanas, 1977.

Lasswell, T. E. *Class and Stratum.* Boston: Houghton-Mifflin, 1965.

Laumann, E. O., and others. *The Logic of Social Hierarchies.* Chicago: Markham Publishers, 1970.

Lawrence, P. R., and J. W. Lorsch. *Organization and Environment: Differentiation and Integration.* Boston: Graduate School of Business Administration, Harvard University, 1967.

Lazarsfeld, P. F. Reflections on Business: Consumers and Managers. Mimeographed paper. Columbia University, Dept. of Sociology, 1959.

Leach, E. *Culture and Communication.* Cambridge: Cambridge University Press, 1976.

Lesser, G. S., and others. Experimental Arousal of Achievement Motivation in Adolescent Girls. *Journal of Abnormal and Social Psychology* 66(1963):59–66.

Lesser, G. S., and others. Mental Abilities of Children from Different Social Class and Cultural Groups. *Monograph of the Society for Research in Child Development* 30 (1965).

LeVine, R. *Culture, Behavior and Personality.* Chicago: Aldine, 1973.

Lewin, K. *Field Theory in Social Science: Selected Theoretical Papers.* London: Tavistock, 1952.

Liebig, James E. *Merchants of Vision.* San Francisco: Berret Koehler, 1994.

Likert, R. *New Ways of Managing Conflict.* New York: McGraw-Hill, 1976.

Lipman-Blumen, J., and H. Leavitt. Vicarious and Direct Achievement Patterns in Adulthood. *The Counseling Psychologist* 6(1):26–32.

Lipset, S. M. *Political Man.* Garden City, NY: Doubleday, 1963.

Littig, L. W. The Effect of Motivation on Probability Preferences and Subjective Probability. Unpublished Ph.D. diss. University of Michigan, 1959.

Littig, L. W., and C. A. Yeracaris. Academic Achievement Correlates of Achievement and Affiliation Motivations. *Journal of Psychology* 55(1963):115–119.

Litwin, G. H. Achievement Motivation, Social Class, and the Slope of Occupational Preferences in the United States and Japan. Dittoed paper. Department of Social Relations, Harvard University, 1959.

Litwin, G. H. Motives and Expectancy as Determinants of Preference for Degrees of Risk. Unpublished honors thesis. University of Michigan, 1958.

Litwin, G. H., and R. A. Stringer. *Motivation and Organizational Climate.* Boston: Graduate School of Business Administration, Harvard University, 1968.

Loevinger, J. The Meaning and Measurement of Ego Development. *American Psychologist* 21(1966):195–206.

Loevinger, J., and others. *Measuring Ego Development (Vol. 2)*. San Francisco: Jossey-Bass, 1970.

Loevinger, J., and Wessler, R. *Measuring Ego Development (Vol. 1)*. San Francisco: Jossey-Bass, 1970.

Loevinger, J. *Ego Development: Conceptions and Theories*. San Francisco: Jossey-Bass, 1976.

Loevinger. J. *Ego Development*. San Francisco: Jossey-Bass, 1978.

Looft, W. Socialization and Personality Throughout the Life-span. In *Life-span Developmental Psychology: Personality and Socialization,* eds. P. Baltes and K. Schaie, 26–52. New York: Academic Press. 1973.

Lowell, E. L. The Effect of Need for Achievement on Learning and Speed of Performance. *Journal of Psychology* 33(1952):31–40.

Lucas, R. Validation of a Test of Ego Development by Means of a Standardized Interview. Ph.D. diss., Washington University, 1971.

Luria, A. R. *Cognitive Development: Its Cultural and Social Foundations*. Cambridge: Harvard University Press, 1976.

Lynn, R. Cross-cultural Differences in Neuroticism, Extraversion and Psychoticism. In *Dimensions of Personality: Papers in Honor*, eds. H. J. Eysenck & R. Lynn, Chapter 12. Oxford: Pergamon, 1981.

Mahone, C. H. Fear of Failure and Unrealistic Vocational Aspiration. *Journal of Abnormal Social Psychology* 60(1960):253–261.

March, J. G., and H. Simon. *Organizations*. New York: Wiley, 1958.

Martin, J. *Cultures in Organizations*. New York: Oxford University Press, 1992.

Martire, J. G. Relationships Between the Self-Concept and Differences in the Strength and Generality of Achievement Motivation. *Journal of Personality* 24(1956):364–375.

Maslow, A. *Motivation and Personality*. New York: Harper, 1954.

Maslow, A. *Towards a Psychology of Being*. Princeton, NJ: Van Nostrand, 1962.

Maslow, A. H. *Motivation and Personality*. New York: Harper & Row, 1970.

McClelland, D. C., and others. *The Achievement Motive*. New York: Appleton-Century-Crofts, 1953.

McClelland, D. C. Risk Taking in Children with High and Low Need for Achievement. In *Motives in Fantasy, Action, and Society*, ed. J. W. Atkinson, 306-321. Princeton: Van Nostrand, 1958.

McClelland, D. C. *The Achieving Society*. Princeton: Van Nostrand Reinhold, 1961.

McClelland, D. C. Towards a Theory of Motive Acquisition. *American Psychologist* 20(5):321–333.

McClelland, D. C. Does Education Accelerate Economic Growth? *Economic Development and Cultural Change* 14(1966):257–278.

McClelland, D. C., and D. G. Winter. *Motivating Economic Achievement*. New York: The Free Press, 1969.

McClelland, D. C. The Two Faces of Power. *Journal of International Affairs* 24(1970):29–47.

McClelland, D. C. *Power, the Inner Experience*. New York: Irvington Publishers, 1975.

McKeachie, W. J. Motivation, Teaching, Methods and College Learning. In *Nebraska Symposium on Motivation*, ed. M. R. Jones, 11–141. Lincoln: University of Nebraska Press, 1961.

Mcluhan, M. *Os Meios de Comunicando Como Extensoes do Homem*. São Paulo: Cultrix, 1969.

Meier, G. M., and R. E. Baldwin. *Economic Development*. New York: Wiley, 1957.

Merbaum, A. D. Need for Achievement in Negro and White Children. Unpublished Ph.D. diss., University of North Carolina, 1962.

Merriam-Webster, Incorporated. *The Merriam-Webster Online Dictionary.* Internet: Merriam-Webster, Incorporated, 2003.

Merton, R. K. *Social Theory and Social Structure.* New York: Free Press, 1968.

Miles, R. E., and C. C. Snow. Causes of Failure in Network Organizations. *California Management Review,* Summer 1992: 53–72.

Morris, M. H., and others. Fostering Corporate Entrepreneurship: Cross-cultural Comparisons of the Importance of Individualism versus Collectivism. *Journal of International Business Studies* 25(1):65–89.

Mueller, C. *The Politics of Communication.* London: Oxford University Press, 1973.

Murray, H. A. *Explorations in Personality.* New York: Oxford University Press, 1938.

Naisbitt, John, and Patricia Aburdene. *Re-inventing the Corporation.* New York: Warner Books, 1985.

Noet, David M. *Healing the Wounds.* San Francisco: Jossey Bass, 1993.

Osterberg, Rolf. *Corporate Renaissance.* Mill Valley, CA: Nataraj Publishing, 1993.

Parnes, Sidney. *Visionizing.* East Aurora, NY: DOK Publishing, 1988.

Parsons, T., and E. A. Shils. *Toward a General Theory of Action.* Cambridge: Harvard University, 1951.

Payne, R. L., and D. S. Pugh. Organization Structure and Climate. In *Handbook of Industrial and Organizational Psychology,* ed. Dunnette, M. D. 1125–1173. Chicago: Rand McNally, 1976.

Perlmutter, H. V. More than 50 Percent of International Managers Time is Spent in Negotiating in Interpersonal Transaction Time Influencing Other Managers. *Academy of Management Meetings. Wharton School, University of Pennsylvania (*1984).

Perls, F. *Gestalt Therapy Verbatim*, ed. J.Wysong, Lafayette. CA: Real People Press, 1969.

Pettigrew, A. M. *The Politics of Organizational Decision-making.* London: Tavistock, 1973.

Piaget, J. *Growth of Logical Thinking.* London: Routledge & Kegan Paul, 1958.

Piaget, J. *Intelligence and Affectivity.* Palo Alto: Annual Reviews, 1981.

Pinedo, Victor Jr. "Loevinger's Ego Stages as the Basis of an Intervention Model." In *The 1978 Annual Handbook for Group Facilitators*, eds. J. William Pfeiffer & John E. Jones. La Jolla: University Associates Press, 1978.

Porter, M. E. *Competitive Strategy: Techniques for Analyzing Industries and Competitors.* New York: Free Press, 1980.

Prahalad, C. K., and Y. Doz. *The Multinational Mission: Balancing Local Demands and Global Vision.* New York: Free Press, 1987.

Reich, Wilhelm. *Charakteranalyse: Technik und Grundlagen.* Vienna: Zelbstverlag (Manzsche, Vienna), 1933.

Rotter, J. B. *Social Learning and Clinical Psychology.* New York: Prentice-Hall, 1954.

Rotter, J. B. Generalized Expectancies for Internal versus External Control of Reinforcement. *Psychological Monographs* 80(1)(Whole No. 609), 1966.

Schein, E. H. The Role of the Founder in Creating Organizational Culture. *Organizational Dynamics* 12(1):13–28.

Schein, E. H. *Organizational Culture and Leadership: a Dynamic View.* London: Jossey-Bass, 1986.

Schein, V. E., and others. Think Manager, Think Male: a Global Phenomenon. *Journal of Organizational Behavior* 17(1996):33–41.

Senge, Peter M. *The Fifth Discipline: The Art & Practice of The Learning Organization.* New York: Currency Doubleday, 1990.

Thomas, David A., and Robin J. Ely. Making Differences Matter: a New Paradigm for Managing Diversity. *Harvard Business Review* 74(5):79–90.

Toffler, Alvin. *Future Shock.* New York: Random House, 1970.

Trompenaars, F., and C. Hampden-Turner. *Riding the Waves of Culture: Understanding Cultural Diversity in Business, 2nd ed.* London: Nicholas Brealey, 1993.

Weber, M. *The Protestant Ethic and the Spirit of Capitalism.* London: George Allen & Unwin, 1930.

Wellins, Richard S., and others. *Empowered Teams: Creating Self-directed Work Groups that Improve Quality, Productivity and Participation.* San Francisco: Jossey Bass, 1991.

978-0-595-30655-8
0-595-30655-1

www.ingramcontent.com/pod-product-compliance
Lightning Source LLC
Chambersburg PA
CBHW030941180526
45163CB00002B/665